I will stand on my guard post
and station myself on the rampart;
and I will keep watch to see
what He will speak to me,
and how I may reply when I am reproved.
Then the LORD answered me and said,
"Record the vision
and inscribe it on tablets,
that the one who reads it may run.
For the vision is yet for the appointed time;
it hastens toward the goal and it will not fail.
Though it tarries, wait for it;
for it will certainly come, it will not delay…"

Habakkuk 2:1–3 (NASB)

Advance Praise for The Overseer

"This important book correctly and compassionately identifies the most frequently missing element in pastoral effectiveness. Pastors who understand and grow in their biblical role as overseers will find churches that not only love and respect them, but that will eagerly follow them in fulfilling the church's mission."

Nate Adams
Executive Director, Illinois Baptist State Association

"In over 40 years of ministering to churches and coaching pastors, I have read many books on leadership and church revitalization. Some I have discarded and some I have kept. This book will stay on my shelf for many years to come. I predict it will become a classic."

Walker Armstrong
Executive Director of Triad Church Network, NC

"In The Overseer, *Rob Peters names the elephant in the room for evangelical pastors worldwide and effectively points to God's call and provision for every pastor to become an effective revitalization leader. This should be required reading for every seminary student and an oft-reviewed reference in every pastor's library."*

Scott Foshie
Health Team Leader, Illinois Baptist State Association

"Apart from God's Word and the Holy Spirit, the greatest single influence on a church is its pastor. As Rob Peters wisely points out, "The biblical role for leaders, as envisioned by Paul and Peter, comprises the three roles of elder, shepherd, and overseer. Most pastors enter the work with more-than-adequate skills as shepherds and elders, but woefully underprepared as overseers (possessing strategic vision and the ability to effect needed change)..."

ENDORSEMENTS

"...The Overseer provides wise counsel to enable pastors to be the skilled overseers their churches need them to be. I highly recommend it."

Ray Gentry
President of Southern Baptist Conference of Associational Leaders

"There is great need today for biblical and practical church revitalization principles. In The Overseer, *Rob Peters answers many pressing questions backed by years of experience, both as a pastor and consultant. Churches will be strengthened, and God's Kingdom advanced by this book."*

Gary Hollingsworth
Executive Director/Treasurer, South Carolina Baptist Convention

"While many have written about the increasing problem, Rob's new book, The Overseer, *provides the best biblical process available for equipping pastors to lead their churches to experience revitalization. He writes as an experienced pastor who has revitalized churches, who has great concern for pastors and the local church, and who has researched and developed a proven strategy for guiding these leaders and churches towards greater health and growth. Readers will find* The Overseer *to be very insightful, encouraging, and practical for their ministries. I heartily recommend this book to pastors!"*

John Horn
Church Health Team Leader, State Convention of Baptists in Indiana

"As I read through The Overseer, *I reflected back to my earlier years of ministry and wished I had this book to guide me back then. Rob Peters takes us on a journey to healthier outcomes through skillful adaptations. I highly recommend it to all church leaders."*

Mark Jones
Pastor & State Convention of Baptists in Ohio Revitalization Consultant

"Rob and I were youth ministry interns together as college students. It has been a joy to watch how the Lord has used him through the years to strengthen the church. I was impressed with how his new book, The Overseer, *is so biblical, practical, and interesting. I highly recommend it to encourage and challenge your ministry."*

Cliff Lea
Senior Pastor, First Baptist Church, Leesburg, Florida

"Rob's skill and wisdom in leadership has benefited me personally as well as churches throughout Missouri. Through The Overseer, *Rob has provided an incredible resource for many other pastors and churches to develop and utilize the critical leadership skills desperately needed in declining congregations. The process and practical tools that fill this work are priceless."*

Brandon Moore, PhD
Resound Network Director for the Missouri Baptist Convention

"I serve a number of pastors who are tired, bewildered, and dejected. They are working at maximum capacity, passionately serving as pastor and teacher, but there are daunting challenges they face as leaders. Pastor, there is help on the horizon. Dr. Rob Peters has stepped in to offer hope and solutions to pastors regardless of the size of the church. In The Overseer, *Rob teaches us to become adaptive leaders who seek God to discern our situation, craft an action plan, communicate a solution, and position our churches for maximum impact."*

Chris Reynolds
Pastor Wellness Catalyst, Georgia Baptist Mission Board

ENDORSEMENTS

"Most pastors know what a thriving church should look like, but many lack the skill set necessary to lead their plateaued church to flourish. In this book, Rob strengthens pastors who feel stuck to develop biblically faithful skills and processes that reposition the church for maximum impact."

James Risner
Associational Missionary, Greater Dayton Association of Baptists

"I am very thankful for Dr. Rob Peters, and I am glad that he has dedicated his wisdom towards Kingdom advancement through the local church. His training, skillset, and practical experience have uniquely equipped him to speak to the issue of pastoral leadership. Rob's approach is biblically grounded, practically informed, and well-illustrated. A pastor's capacity for adaptive leadership is critical and this text sets a path to develop that capacity. I pray that pastors and associational leaders will utilize this resource to enhance and better serve the church."

Todd Robertson
Associational Mission Strategist, Louisville Regional Baptist Association

"Dr. Peters combines a wealth of experience, leadership wisdom, and biblical insight to help pastors gain a fresh perspective on their role and responsibility in leading their church. Peters guides the reader step by step through the journey to a more vital and healthy church. This book is full of practical guidance to help churches fulfill the Great Commission."

Steffen Schulte
Rector of Rhineland School of Theology

ENDORSEMENTS

"Pastor, if you are discouraged because everything you have tried has not revitalized your church, then you must read this book! Rob Peters draws on his 25 years of pastoring and consulting churches to teach you how to develop the vital role of overseer. He shares practical principles and tools that will equip and empower pastors to refocus and revitalize their churches."

Rusty Sumrall
Church Consultant & Lead Coach, Nashville Baptist Association

"The Overseer is far more than just another book on leadership; it is a book that provides a biblical context to the specific adaptive leadership skills needed by pastors leading revitalization in their church. Dr. Rob Peters' heart and vision for church revitalization offers real hope and real solutions to this tremendous need."

Tommy Thompson
Lead Pastor, Ashburn Baptist Church, Chicago, IL

"The Overseer offers a comprehensive and practical set of blueprints on how to be a more effective Kingdom leader. Rob offers a vast array of insightful and instructive experiences fused with wise observations that overflow with Holy Spirit-guided wisdom. I highly recommend this valuable volume to anyone on the leadership spectrum ranging from rookie to the elder Christian statesman. Implementing Rob's leadership lessons will help you equip the saints to do the work of ministry, advance Christ's Kingdom, and sleep better at night. Rob's work is destined to become a classic in the field of church leadership that will glorify God and bring great good to His people."

Jay Wolf
Pastor Emeritus, First Baptist Church Montgomery, AL

THE
OVERSEER

THE OVERSEER

THE MISSING JEWEL IN THE CROWN OF GLORY

DR. ROB PETERS

To Gene Mims

The first time I saw an overseer in action, you were leading the staff of the First Baptist Church of Cleveland, Tennessee, putting together a playbook to help every ministry work together to fulfill the mission of the church. I did not understand at the time all you were teaching me, but thank you for showing and then telling me what to do as an overseer. You also challenged me to complete my accounting degree after God called me to ministry. You said, "Trust me, you will use it more than you know." Your wisdom has shaped my life and ministry.

To Tony Golding

Every one of these steps was hammered out in conversation with you. Usually, it was on the golf course, so thankfully we had something other than my golf game to talk about. Your patient listening, insightful questions, and practical ideas all helped to simplify, clarify, and focus my thinking. You also believed in me and what God put in my heart; so much so, that you launched this ministry with me. Thank you for your investment in me and in Corpus and thank you for sharing so much of my life with me.

Contents

Preface

I remember the day so very well. It was a cold day and I was at home, studying for Sunday's sermon while my wife was at school teaching second graders. The sun was shining, but it was chilly outside in the burgeoning northern suburbs of Atlanta.

Our little church, which had been replanted from another failed church plant, had been struggling to gain momentum. With time, prayer, hard work, and a lot of really skilled people leading beside me, that little church began to grow. We had purchased property, put up an initial temporary facility, and started our work towards a master plan for the eighteen acres of property we had purchased and paid off.

I remember very well the conversation that day with Dr. Lea. My confession came easily: "Dr. Lea, I don't know what I am doing." I remember his kind, Virginia laugh on the other end. "Rob, what do you mean you don't know what you are doing? You won the pastoral leadership award the faculty gives to a deserving recipient from the student body." I wanted to confess that I was not worthy of that award, but the words came out differently. Instead, I said, "Dr. Lea, I know how to do all the things you and my other professors taught me to do, but what I don't know how to do is lead these people forward together towards God's desired future."

I thought at the time that I was the only seminary student who had ever felt that way, but what I learned over the years through many honest and vulnerable conversations is that almost all pastors at one time or another struggle with the same thing. Dr. Lea was kind to counsel and to connect me. He connected me to a Dallas Theological Seminary professor named Aubrey Malphurs. My relationship with Dr. Malphurs proved to be a turning point in my ministry, unlocking for me so many leadership insights and eventually preparing me to pursue leadership insights for myself.

While I struggled with many of the frameworks Dr. Malphurs established, I felt safe within them, because he was a theologian by training, and his heart was so pure. He said to me one day, "Rob when you are no longer confined by my framework for thinking, you are going to make a great contribution to the field of church leadership." I don't know if I will ever live up to his prophetic language or not, but I do remember the day when I no longer felt confined to the "General Revelation" category that Dr. Malphurs uses in the introduction of so many of his works.

I remember the day so well when the "skills" I had been learning and the study of scripture that I had been undertaking moved from what I would call "skill" to "art." I no longer felt confined to other people's models as I moved off the map of what had already been written about a field of study that was truly new and exciting. I felt that I began doing in church leadership what Paul did when he preached where no one had previously preached.

I was sitting on my back porch in North Carolina, reading 1 Peter devotionally. I was reading from my pocket New Testament, which happened to be the New King James Version. I usually only used this version for many of the funeral services for older church members. But, since I had just come home from performing a funeral, I was reading from it when I stumbled across the words I had never noticed before: "Jesus is the Great Overseer."

I had been tinkering with the fact that the two leading apostles both presented the triad of elder—shepherd—overseer as a model for young pastors to follow. Paul used this framework in Acts 20 and Peter uses it more succinctly in 1 Peter 5. I had been thinking about the fact that the two leading apostles used this framework and that the deficiency in modern seminary education was not in the eldership function nor in that of pastoral care, but in the overseer role, where leadership, assessment, repositioning, vision casting, strategy, leadership development, and execution resided. This discovery sent me into a full-on search mode to know more.

I had known Dr. Warren Gage from my time in south Florida, and his extensive work in typology had helped unpack what was a line of study in seminary that proved to be somewhat profitable. Taking some of the techniques I learned from seminary and others from this new friend with whom I shared a similar church background, I began my pursuit. One of the most enlightening moments early in my struggle with this concept came when I had the privilege of working beside a church revitalization team put together by an Associational Mission Strategist (AMS). It just so happened that Todd Robertson led the team in a city that is significant to Southern Baptists because Louisville is home to Southern Baptists' oldest seminary. While at the table that day I had gathered with a professor leading church revitalization, a leading Hebrew scholar, and a director of church missions. Also at the table was Brian Croft, the founder of Practical Shepherding. Needless to say, the conversations and lines of thought that I was able to pursue were illuminated that day. The final sentence spoken to me that day by Brian included him saying, "Rob, I can truly see a clear lane of study for you in this field, and I am so glad God has opened this door for you to enrich the church." I am sure those speaking at the event that day did not realize the monumental nature of that moment in the course of Corpus's ministry, but I can tell you there was a clear path paved before me in the work we were undertaking.

PREFACE

What you will find in this work is a collection of failure, wrestling, discovery, conversation, refinement, experimentation, and improvement. All of this work has been done across five continents and many different denominations. This has created what I refer to as a universal application of the overseer skillsets. All of these are rooted in biblical principles lived out in real-life situations through biblical characters and then captured for us in the canon of scripture. The result is a set of timeless truths, not trendy new lingo applied to recycled business principles.

I can assure you that you will never fail at the application of these principles more than I have, but I hope in wrestling with these revealed truths and biblical concepts that you will experience the shift I made as I discovered and practiced them. I shifted from the posture that I need something to help me organize, lead, and facilitate the work of the church, to a posture of confidence in God's prescribed plan for doing the work of the ministry. I shifted from, "I think I need principles and a philosophy" to "God has given me principles and a philosophy," and I took on His mandate for effective and biblical leadership as I began to practice these truths and as the church benefited from following God's design.

My hope is you are already on your own journey of learning and discovery. Part of your learning probably has been out of necessity; some of it may have been models imported from other disciplines. I believe, like Aubrey Malphurs, that those models can be used. But one thing I am convinced of is that there is a clear, fully biblical model for giving oversight to the church, one that God has mandated and that He will bless. It will be for the good of pastors and it will bring Him glory in the church because God is the one who originated it.

As I draw these thoughts to a close, let me invite you to make this book the first of several steps in your journey toward being a faithful overseer. There are any number of steps you can take that will continue to develop you as an overseer, but here are a few you might want to consider that Corpus has designed its ministry to facilitate.

1. Take the step of connecting with a Corpus-certified coach to help you assess your personal skills as a wise elder, a skilled overseer, and a transformational shepherd. *You can visit www.corpusvitae.org/assessments to learn more.*

2. Take the step of being a certified Overseer by attending a two-day event where you will learn more about the overseer

skills and learn how to implement all six skills into your ministry. *Learn more at www.theoverseer.info*

3. Take the step of being a Certified Transitional Revitalization Pastor so you can help churches without a pastor launch the work of church revitalization. *See www.corpusvitae.org/events.*

4. Take the step of becoming a multiplier of the work of the overseer and create movement in your networks or denominations. You can do this by becoming a certified coach or pathfinder who will both teach the principles of the overseer and coach individual pastors to effectively implement them in their ministries.

The church has been more anemic than it needed to be for far too long. Pastors have groped in the darkness when it came to church leadership, wondering what was permissible to use and what they should avoid. But now the time has come for the church to have pastors who deploy the full range of resources God has designed for them to have in their toolkit. The roles of elder and shepherd have rightfully gotten the necessary attention these important roles have needed in the last five decades. However, now is the time to give the role of the overseer its rightful place in the triad of effective pastoral leadership.

One final word I want to share about the book's title. *The Overseer* is obvious. What may not be so obvious is the subtitle: *The Missing Jewel in the Crown of Glory*. It was A. W. Tozer who raised the question in chapter one of *The Knowledge of the Holy*, then later came back and wrote the book titled *Worship: The Missing Jewel*. These words and the ideas they shaped so influenced me that, when it came time to write this work, the idea rang in my mind so clearly that there was nothing else to consider but Tozer's expression applied to the work of the overseer. Pastors, there is a missing jewel. You, like me, have probably been trained inside the matrix of a well-honed formula for equipping pastors for ministry. And while there are many redeeming qualities that all of us have taken from that formula, there is no doubt that one part of the equation has been left undeveloped. My prayer and deepest longing are that this work will in some way contribute to the larger body of work in a way that pastors and churches have so desperately needed.

His and yours,

Dr. Rob Peters
Winter 2023

Scan the QR Code to learn more about Corpus resources and training events. Videos describing the Corpus ministry and the ReFocus process for revitalization are available here on our website.

Acknowledgments

The work you hold in your hands is my Corpus. One definition of "Corpus" is "a collection of written texts, especially the entire works of a particular author or a body of writing on a particular subject." While I know there is more to learn in the field of study about being and becoming an overseer, this book contains what 30-plus years of local church ministry have taught me.

I am excited to share with you my first comprehensive expression of what I have learned thus far about the biblical concept of an overseer. This effort at identifying the theological underpinnings, the biblical typology, and the practical pastoral and ecclesiological implications has been 30 years in the making. There are many people to thank as this project comes to its first conclusion.

First to my wife, Wendy, and children, Anna Grace, John, and Liam: I am so grateful to live life in the crucible of growth and learning called my family. Your patient love and tolerance of my constant need to learn more, talk more, and discover more has encouraged me and the ministry of Corpus more than you can know. Your love, kidding, and inspiration are something I carry with me every day, no matter where I find myself.

There are many people to thank for teaching, coaching, and investing in me who have in some way contributed to this work. Let me very succinctly sketch out the path as I have thus far recognized it.

My father, Robert "Joe" Peters, taught me about continuous process improvement and the work of Tom Peters and Edwards Deming. He coached me every day to be a little better and more of what God created me to be.

Dr. Gene Mims demonstrated for me what an overseer was before I even knew what that meant.

John Coxwell, a partner with the Deloitte accounting and consulting firm, along with my college accounting professors, Dr. Cook, Dr. Fessler, and Dr. Swanson, all encouraged me to explore ministry, even while giving me unlimited opportunities in the accounting field.

C. W. Brister entrusted me with an award named after his work at Southwestern Seminary. He came closest in seminary to teaching pastors these truths and always listened and considered the ramblings of a seminary student.

Dr. Tommy Lea recognized what a pastor was asking and introduced me to Dr. Aubrey Malphurs, whose works, writings, and personal coaching influenced me more than he ever knew.

ACKNOWLEDGMENTS

Bob Bumgarner, Will Mancini, and Steve Stroope coached me regularly and challenged my thoughts and ideas about leading within the church context.

Additionally, the Corpus board has been influential in helping shape and support what Corpus has become today. Thank you to Frank Byrne, Jerry Mellinger, Jeff Mims, Abner Wright, Mark Nash, and Russell Barnes, our active board members at the time of publication. Also, thank you to Fred Kremkau and Gary Baldwin, who have served on the Corpus board.

Two people made special contributions to this work as they helped me overcome my handicaps in written expression to articulate these biblical truths, the practical applications, and the stories that convey the practical outcomes of being an overseer: Greg Webster and Thom Lemmons.

Special thanks to our Corpus core team, Greg Poss, Melanie Patton, Betsy Sprickman, and Joy LaLiberte. Special thanks are also extended to Tammy Priest, who worked tirelessly, early in our Corpus development, to give the initial shape to our efforts to bring these truths to those who needed them most.

Finally, to the practitioners in the field who have helped deliver and implement the overseer concepts most and best: Joey Rodgers, Scott Foshie, Steffen Schulte, and Alexandre Antoine. Your constant experimentation, conversation, and courage to try inspires me. You are true kingdom leaders. There are countless other local associational leaders, state convention servants, and denominational leaders all over the world who have helped shape these concepts into what they are today.

To each of these people and to so many more who deserve to have their contribution acknowledged, I express my deep gratitude for their work, which is now helping the church "ReFocus."

THE
OVERSEER

Introduction

Why didn't anyone ever teach me that?

In consulting with churches for the past 25 years, it's the most common question I hear from pastors. They wonder why no one ever taught them the skills needed to be a competent leader. The question is not always spoken out loud, but it is almost always there. Most pastors know, deep down, that they've not been prepared by seminary, Bible college, or any other formal training to *lead* a congregation.

I also know the painful effects of this lack of training from my own personal experience. I was once one of those pastors asking why no one taught me to lead.

Had you known me back then, you might have thought I had my ministry act completely together. Certainly, the external indicators said so. At Southwestern Seminary (the world's largest seminary at the time), I had won the C. W. Brister Pastoral Leadership Award. But a year into pastoring my first church, internal alarms were screaming, telling me I was on a collision course with total ministry failure. I realized I didn't know how to take my congregation where it needed to go, and I was desperate for help.

So, I called Dr. Lea, the dean of theology at Southwestern and one of my mentors. I confessed to him that I didn't know what I was doing.

He said to me: "Rob, if *you* don't know what you're doing, then we're not doing a very good job."

"Don't get me wrong," I responded, "I know how to preach a sermon, share the gospel, do a funeral, make hospital visits, and perform weddings. What I don't know is how to lead a group of people to work together on God's mission."

His final words stunned me but explained precisely why I—and now I know, others—was in crisis: "Well, Rob, we really don't teach pastors how to do that here at Southwestern."

This is not to suggest that there was something particularly wrong at Southwestern Seminary. To the contrary, Dr. Lea's explanation would have been typical of seminaries all over the country. Countless pastors have been left to wonder why no one taught them how to lead. Yet, when you consider all the Bible has to say about leadership, it's an odd problem.

The Missing Overseer

According to Scripture, leadership in the church means that a pastor is an overseer, but few church "leaders" actually fulfill that role. At its core, the concept of overseer involves stewardship, vision-casting, organizing, administrating, and other skills required when a large, diverse, and growing number of people (i.e., a church) are pursuing a specific goal, and these are the skills seminaries don't teach.

The Bible says there are three primary roles a pastor's job can be divided into—elder, shepherd, and overseer—and seminaries do a great job of teaching the first two. Nearly every minute of a student's time is spent learning something about how to teach (the job of an elder) or how to shepherd a "flock." Hardly a second, though, is spent on leadership.

Why?

Largely because "leadership" skills seem worldly to many Christians. They include elements like devising strategy, setting goals, casting a vision, articulating core values, creating an organizational culture, and raising up other leaders. To some, these sound like "secular" business practices and as a result, they feel there's no place for them in the church. Most seminarians, in fact, are happy with this mix of teaching because they're not in full-time ministry yet so they haven't grasped the significance of leadership skills. And as for the misperception that these ideas are "secular": They don't realize that God uses these aspects of leadership and that the Bible taught these practices long before modern business principles were anywhere on the radar of history (more about this in the next section).

Because pastors are not taught to lead effectively, many are desperately frustrated by their calling—so many that 90 percent of all pastors who leave the ministry do so because they feel like a failure in the overseer role. Pastors are smart and care deeply about their people, but they don't know how to implement leadership practices that would enhance the teaching and nurturing of their people. They even have an aversion to these practices because they are largely outside of their comfort zone or seem "unspiritual."

The problem is made worse by the massive decline in church participation. Studies show that of the 400,000 churches in the United States, 75 to 90 percent are in some level of decline—in membership, financial stability, vitality, or effective ministry. Of the declining churches, about 72 give up and close their doors every week (as of this writing, more than 3,700 every year!).

More than ever, this is the exact environment that calls for leaders to step up and fully execute the role of overseer. Churches need leaders who can assess what's happening around them and lead the changes required to fulfill the church's mission.

The Promise of the Skilled Overseer

The Apostle Peter offers a powerful and concise overview of the need for pastors to mesh their three biblical roles of elder, shepherd, and overseer. In 1 Peter 5:1–3, he says:

> *Therefore, I urge **elders** among you, as your fellow elder and a witness of the sufferings of Christ, and one who is also a fellow partaker of the glory that is to be revealed: **shepherd** the flock of God among you, exercising **oversight**, not under compulsion but voluntarily, according to the will of God; and not with greed but with eagerness; nor yet as domineering over those assigned to your care, but by proving to be examples to the flock (emphasis mine).*

The three roles are connected, and it's important to think through how they work together.

To teach well, an elder must be wise in his grasp of the Faith, and to shepherd a flock, the pastor must love people and help them become like Jesus. Yet these two roles take place within an organization of diverse individuals who can create havoc without the right oversight. Here's where the overseer role comes in. A skilled overseer will orchestrate a healthy culture *within* the church, so it becomes a place where disciples grow in Christ and fulfill His mission.

Leadership skills make possible the long-term growth of people in a congregation. And as individuals grow, churches grow—sidestepping the otherwise near certain destiny of decay and decline.

Leadership of this sort—especially in times like we live in—requires a resilience to endure and make right judgments about what to do next. It necessitates a specific skill called *adaptive leadership*.

Not everything works out each day the way we hope it will, let alone over years in the life of a church. An adaptive leader knows how to make reasonable and effective plans for his church by first adapting to whatever the church's current situation is. He also recognizes the need for change along the way. Good plans are essential for success, but no plan perfectly anticipates all that can happen in the future. So, adaptation is required along the way and can turn the angst of change into the joy of opportunity.

Finally, skilled leadership opens the door to a personal benefit for the pastor who leads well. The fourth verse in the 1 Peter 5 passage explains what's in store for effective church leaders: "And when the Chief Shepherd appears, *you will receive the unfading crown of glory*" (NASB, emphasis mine).

For overseers who have done their job well, God promises a "crown of glory"—a heavenly reward. Although we may not know exactly what that crown will be like, it certainly sounds like no pastor would want to miss out on the jewel-in-the-crown offered for being a good overseer.

To Plant or Revive?

You might wonder if the sort of adaptive leadership we're talking about is already in play through the excellent church planting and church growth practices that have been implemented over the past several decades. It can be tempting to think that better implementation of church growth strategies can solve the problem of declining churches, but unfortunately, that isn't working.

Church growth specialists Warren Byrd and Ed Stetzer show that 4,000 churches are planted every year, and about 3,400 survive more than five years. That means more churches are closing every year in America (over 3,700, remember?) than are being successfully planted. So, the problem isn't that the work of church planting is failing. In fact, the numbers suggest great success in getting churches started. The problem is the failure rate, and solving that requires a different approach.

That approach is called *revitalization.*

Yet, church revitalization calls upon the very leadership skills that seminaries don't teach and pastors don't easily embrace. The overseer role is *the* key to revitalization. Revitalization requires intense change management and culture-shifting, combined with high-powered people and organizational skills. Hence, the work of church revitalization requires a different type of leadership. It is not strictly visionary leadership, nor is it simply managerial leadership. Revitalization calls for adaptive leadership.

Leadership of this sort requires a resilience to endure and make right judgments about what to do next—then make correct judgments about how to adapt to the next changes that occur. The challenges faced when doing revitalization demand the skills of the overseer. And the really good news is that any pastor can learn the overseer skill set. That's the purpose of this book—helping you embrace the skill set needed to lead a church into revitalization.

Here's a summary of what an adaptive leader must do to revitalize his church (the things we'll be discussing in the pages that follow):

◊ Accurately assess the church;

◊ Rightly position the church;

◊ Clearly cast vision;

◊ Multiply disciples;

◊ Rally other leaders;

◊ Effectively execute plans.

Handling all those musts is a tall order, and there is no silver bullet to make it easy. Yet handling the role is immensely doable for those who grasp the essentials of what it means to be a biblical overseer.

I'll say it again: Each of these skills can be learned. *And you can learn them!*

If you do, the rewards are remarkable. My experience has shown that even among seriously declining churches, 40 to 60 percent of them can be set on a path to growth and vitality. There are cultural issues within each church, personal issues with each pastor, and support structures that need to be in place, all of which determine the likelihood of success, but those are part of what we'll be exploring. First, though, let me explain one of the means by which we'll look at the overseer role.

A Story to Tell

In decades of consulting with churches and pastors, I've encountered most every issue and challenge imaginable. They're as varied as the number of churches I've helped, and yet striking similarities have driven me to scripture to discover universal biblical principles expressed through practical church resources and tools. What I have discovered is that pastors worldwide are dealing with similar challenges and have little more than imported, practical, and secular principles to draw upon for help.

To plumb the depths of the spiritual, emotional, administrative, and relational issues involved in revitalizing a church, I've created three different pastoral "characters" who represent situations I've seen repeated time and time and time again. Beginning in chapter 1, I'll set up the narratives of three pastors who reflect how things are in many churches.

By sharing the stories of these folks, I'm not giving away any specific person's secrets. None of the characters are "real" in the sense that I'm basing them on particular individuals I've known. But I can assure you, they are all very real in that I've seen their issues in countless pastors and churches. To arrive at solutions for the three characters, I'll speak to each situation the way I would to a church with which I'm consulting.

You will likely see something of yourself and your situation in at least one of the pastor types I describe. I hope so. Because when you identify with the circumstances I share, you'll be on your way to discovering how revitalization can happen in your specific setting. You'll discover a new confidence and competence to handle leadership challenges and leave behind self-doubt and uncertainty about your role. In short, you'll love the new skills that make you feel like you can truly succeed in *all three* of your ministry roles.

PART
1

Open Up to
God's Leadership

CHAPTER
1

Embrace the Role of Overseer

Bob Dunbar—Pastor Bob—clicked his office door shut and let the smile dissolve from his face. Head drooping, he walked slowly across plush carpet and slumped into the chair behind his desk. He pushed taut fingers through his thick, graying hair and sighed deeply.

Like every Sunday, he relished the compliments heaped upon his sermon at Grace Community Church, but also like every Sunday, three or four dozen came with burning requests for a personal meeting with him. Perhaps 30 or 40 wasn't too bad for a congregation of 2,600, but it was too many for him to handle. So, as always, he told them to contact his secretary to "set something up," and, as always, he knew she would diligently put off all but the most strident requests.

And the tsunami of notes and requests from his staff? Opening the computer to check email all but triggered chest pains for him. The charisma that built his mega-church was no longer enough to get by on.

Sometime in the next hour, though, Pastor Bob would head home to spend Sunday afternoon crafting a few words for that evening's service at Grace, but first, he needed time just to stare at the walls.

A Timeless Theological Framework

Desperate pastors get desperate most often because their position demands something they're not prepared to give. It's not that they don't want to give all their people need. After all, if their calling is about anything, it's about giving to God and His people. The problem isn't that they *won't*; it's that they *can't* give what is needed.

Regardless of church size or length of time in ministry, most pastors lack the skills to lead effectively because, as we discussed in the introduction, no one has ever trained them to do it. And most often, they haven't been taught because of the dysfunctional perception that "business-like" leadership skills are unbecoming of a church and its pastor.

I grieve over that attitude, not just because it undermines the potential for churches to accomplish God's mission (though it definitely does), but even more, because it simply is not true that leadership skills are "secular." To underscore the wrong-headedness of thinking that only businesspeople should exhibit certain leadership competencies, we need to look at the Bible.

Our English word "overseer" derives from the Greek term *episkopos*. You may be familiar with its use in the New Testament through the letters of Paul, but the Old Testament, too, has a lot to say about overseers. In the Septuagint, the Greek translation of the Old Testament, *episkopos* is used seventeen times. But, as a leading Hebrew scholar at the largest evangelical Christian seminary in North America shared with me, the role of the overseer was fulfilled by most of the recorded Old Testament leaders, even if they weren't specifically referred to by that term. In fact, the word "overseer" conveys powerful images for a pastor leading revitalization. Derivatives of the word *episkopos* are used to communicate the ideas "to look upon," "to visit," "to consider," "to repair," "to restore," "and "to take leadership responsibility for."

While the descriptions of several Old Testament persons include the term "overseer," the three especially poignant examples are Joseph, Josiah, and Nehemiah. I'll have even more to say about them later, but let me give you an overview of how they demonstrate the type of leadership often lacking in the church.

Joseph exemplifies the quality of a leader who can face his own shortcomings. Early in his life as a visionary, Joseph shared vision in some highly inappropriate ways—poorly enough that his brothers became angry with him and sold him into slavery, just to get rid of him and his offensive approach. Similarly, some pastors grab hold of a vision but hammer people with it in such a way as to drive them away rather than inspire them with it. Joseph repented of his abominable approach and learned to credit God with his vision—and the outcome.

Josiah discovered how far Judah had strayed from the laws of God and immediately set about to correct what had gone wrong. He grasped the big-picture problem and developed a detailed strategy for addressing complex issues facing the nation (2 Kings 22 and 2 Chronicles 34). Although he was intimately involved in many corrective measures, Josiah also recognized the limits of what one man—even the king—could accomplish. So, he enlisted other leaders to implement his plans. Josiah was the chief overseer and he appointed other overseers to be responsible for his intended reforms.

Nehemiah envisioned rebuilding the devastated walls of Jerusalem (Nehemiah 1, 2). After assessing the needs of the city, he designed his vision, clearly communicated it to his followers, and crafted a detailed plan to implement it. He also recognized that the revitalization of Jerusalem required not only rebuilding the walls surrounding the city but also cultivating the culture of the city of Jerusalem. Finally, he set the people up for long-term success by preparing other leaders who would follow in his footsteps as overseers after he returned to Persia.

The Triad of Influence

The overseers we meet in the pages of Scripture also had three underlying essentials going for them:

Content. Passion. Character.

In the throes of revitalization, the mettle of a leader will be tested in the extreme, and without the threefold underpinning of right content, deep passion, and sound character for the job, a leader is bound to fail. I call these three components the "Triad of Influence." They are the essence of a leader that, over time, will become the keys to persuading followers to make the changes demanded for the health of the church.

Like Joseph, Josiah, and Nehemiah, most pastors are zealous to do God's work. And zeal is extremely important. Heartfelt passion is what drives a person toward something of significance. The Greek term *pathos* expresses this motivation to do whatever is needed to accomplish a great purpose.

Yet, passion is only one of three essentials a leader must have *within* himself. Passion is supported on either side by the other critical components: content and character.

The Greek term *logos* indicates the substance or *content* of a message or goal. Joseph knew a famine was coming. Josiah realized Israel's godly legacy had derailed and that they would never be restored without getting their focus on God back on track. Nehemiah recognized that Jerusalem's recovery and safety required a wall.

Likewise, pastors must know where they are leading the church they pastor. Their own passion and commitment are the foundation for revitalization among the people they lead.

Joseph, Josiah, and Nehemiah also demonstrate the strength of *character* necessary to lead well. Joseph showed his unwillingness to compromise God's law when he rejected the advances of Potiphar's wife. Nehemiah's bold request of the king—to return to Jerusalem—demonstrated his commitment to doing right regardless of the personal consequences. Josiah single-handedly stood against the tide of godlessness that had infected Jewish society. An uncompromising commitment to God's truth, moral purity, and doing right at all costs is the character required of a godly leader.

As we consider the attributes essential to being an effective overseer, let's take a closer look at the overseers presented to us in scripture. After all, God's people have always needed the overseers whom God has raised up, just as they need them today. We will do well to learn from the patterns we observe as they are recorded in the Bible.

The Biblical Typology of the Overseer

The six essential skillsets of the overseer correspond with the six steps in the church revitalization process, as shown below.

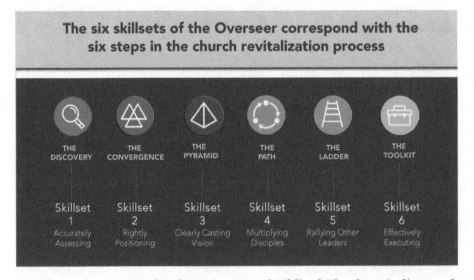

The six skillsets of the Overseer correspond with the six steps in the church revitalization process

THE DISCOVERY	THE CONVERGENCE	THE PYRAMID	THE PATH	THE LADDER	THE TOOLKIT
Skillset 1 Accurately Assessing	Skillset 2 Rightly Positioning	Skillset 3 Clearly Casting Vision	Skillset 4 Multiplying Disciples	Skillset 5 Rallying Other Leaders	Skillset 6 Effectively Executing

The *Baker Evangelical Dictionary of Biblical Theology* indicates that the word "overseer" "... is used a limited number of times in the New Testament, but it has significant implications for a proper understanding of leadership in the church." One of these uses occurs in 1 Peter 2:25, where Jesus is referred to as "the Overseer (Gr., *episkopos*) of your souls" (ESV). A review of biblical sources reveals that this typology is developed in depth in the Old Testament, with rich implications about what an overseer really is and does.

The stories of six characters in the Old Testament intersect with the Old Testament language related to being an overseer. Certainly, there are more than six persons in the Old Testament who perform the work of providing oversight, but these specific characters offer insights into providing leadership for God's people that are explicitly articulated using the word "overseer" or "oversight."

These characters include Eleazar, Joash, Hezekiah, Joseph, Josiah, and Nehemiah. Because of the lengths of their stories and the nature of their work, I find it helpful to refer to them in two groups: minor overseers and major overseers.

The minor overseers are *Eleazar* and *Joash*. Eleazar had oversight of the tabernacle, and his story is told in Numbers 3. He had oversight of those leading in the work of the tabernacle and also oversight of the work being performed. Given the nature of the requirements God established for the tabernacle, this was a job assignment both vital and detailed, requiring knowledge, care, and precision. Eleazar demonstrated two specific skills of an overseer: first, he captured God's vision for the tabernacle and how it would function for God's chosen people; and second, he effectively executed the requirements God laid down for the operation of the tabernacle. Interestingly, of the six overseers under discussion, Eleazar alone did not also lead revitalization. Rather, Eleazar was one of the original leaders of a new work God was initiating among his people. All the other overseers of the Old Testament were revitalizers who sought to restore something that had been lost.

Joash, the other minor overseer, had oversight of the repairs to the temple, as related in 2 Kings 12. His story features the "chest of Joash," which was filled with the necessary resources to pay for the repairs. The story actually begins twenty-three years earlier, when Joash had the vision for the repairs. The priests in charge kept collecting money but failed to repair the temple. Joash challenged this culture of waste and misuse and placed his chest in the temple. He collected the resources, placed those in charge who could accomplish the work, and was said to have dealt faithfully with all the Lord entrusted to him. Joash demonstrated that he had vision, knew how to develop leaders, and executed effectively the tasks of oversight.

The major overseers are *Joseph, Hezekiah, Josiah,* and *Nehemiah.* In these four lives, we see particularly vivid examples of how overseers lead God's people on the path of restoration. While their specific circumstances and challenges varied drastically, these overseers all demonstrated the six key skillsets of an adaptive leader:

1. The ability to accurately assess the needs of a situation;

2. The competence to rightly position a group of people for renewal;

3. The insight to clearly cast vision for followers;

4. The capacity to multiply disciples of their vision;

5. The facility to rally other leaders to the cause;

6. The skill to effectively execute a detailed action plan.

Joseph's story is told in Genesis, chapters 39–50, but the portions specifically addressing Joseph as an overseer are in Genesis 39 and 41. We know Joseph today principally because of his God-given sense of vision, though time and difficult circumstances were required to help Joseph learn to apply his vision in appropriate ways. As a young man, he offended both his brothers and his parents through improper use of his gift for vision-casting, demonstrating a lack of skill in employing his abilities.

As the overseer of Potiphar's house, Joseph made certain advances in his vision-casting abilities that resulted in the blessing and advancement of his master's estate. But Joseph still had to be completely emptied of his pride and self-sufficiency before he was fully usable to God. After languishing in confinement for years, Joseph's skills as an overseer were fully honed and on display when he stood before Pharaoh. Led by God's spirit, Joseph interpreted Pharaoh's dream and developed a clear and compelling plan for saving the known world of that day—including Israel. Joseph demonstrated each of the six essential skills of 1) accurately assessing, 2) rightly repositioning, 3) clearly casting vision, 4) developing the strategy, 5) building leaders, and 6) executing effectively. Joseph is thus the first fully developed overseer presented in this biblical typology; his leadership in the revitalization of Egypt and the surrounding nations is undeniable.

As king, Hezekiah had oversight of Israel, Jerusalem, and the temple. His story is told in 2 Chronicles 29–32 and 2 Kings 18–20. He enacted religious reforms that included the exclusive worship of God and prohibited the worship of other gods. Many of the prophets spoke about the transformation Hezekiah brought about, including his purification of the temple and reformation of the priesthood. Hezekiah was an overseer who had a vision; he repositioned Israel for a generation, developed a strategy for making it happen, built leaders to see the work through, and effectively executed his plan.

Josiah's story is told in 2 Kings 22 and 2 Chronicles 34. King Josiah led the revitalization of his nation, perhaps the greatest Old Testament revival of all. He had the vision to see a complete spiritual renewal in the Jewish people. King Josiah reestablished the temple worship, reinstituted the public reading of scripture, restored God-ordained leadership within the homes of his people, and reinstated the rightful sacrificial system in Jerusalem, according to God's design. For five decades, Josiah's reforms held, maintaining a climate of wholesome spirituality in Israel. Like Joseph, Josiah demonstrated the six skills of 1) accurate assessment, 2) right repositioning, 3) clarity of vision, 4) strategic development, 5) formation and advancement of other leaders, and 6) effective execution.

Finally, Nehemiah is presented as the last of the Old Testament revitalizers and the one who would put in place the things needed to prepare Jerusalem for the eventual arrival of the Messiah. The use of the word "overseer" in Nehemiah's story is not where you might think it would belong in the story, when he is rebuilding the walls. Rather, its use in Nehemiah occurs long after the walls have been rebuilt, when Nehemiah looks around and realizes there is a need to rebuild the culture of the city of Jerusalem. This entailed a long look at what needed to be done in Jerusalem in order to sustain what was necessary for the city of Jerusalem to thrive. Nehemiah certainly drew upon his skills as an overseer throughout his life and ministry. He also demonstrated all of the six skills of the overseer: 1) accurate assessment, 2) right repositioning, 3) clarity of vision, 4) specific strategy, 5) building leaders, and 6) effective execution.

The stories of these overseers are meant not only to serve as inspiration for those who seek to perform the work of the overseer today; they also reveal to us the actual work and activities of an overseer, along with their practical outcomes for God's unfolding vision. The set of skills possessed by each of these overseers gives us a better understanding of what our work as overseers must entail. Overseers today must be able to diagnose problems and challenges. They must know how to reposition churches when change needs to occur. Overseers today must have a plan to lead. They must have the courage to lead, even when there is a price to pay. Today's overseers must lead the actual change and remain courageous in the face of challenges. Overseers today must lead cultural change among the people, even when the people themselves cannot see what they have become or why the culture needs to change.

The Church Had It First

The biblical background for implementing overseer skills is clear. Many heroes in the Old Testament were explicitly referred to as overseers, and their example provides the mandate and example for pastors to do likewise in their churches. There is a grouping of skill sets to accomplish their revitalizing work, and I refer to this as the *Irreducible Minimums of Revitalization Leadership.* Overseer skills are required to do the work of God, especially when revitalization is involved. Unless a leader grasps the vision God has for His people and has the competencies needed to take a congregation where God directs, the mission will fail or be severely and unnecessarily limited.

Since scripture shows these skills at work in God's plan for history, we shouldn't be ambivalent about employing adaptive leadership principles in a church. The church had the background, the examples to follow, and the mandate for ministry success centuries before "modern management principles" were "discovered" by business leaders.

God designed people to be led in the way scripture demonstrates, and it falls to the pastor to tap into the spiritual patterns God has established. People can't join in the mission if they don't know what they're doing—and why and how. Without effective overseers, churches will continue to do what they're doing far too often in the twenty-first century—declining into irrelevance.

Ministry came naturally to James Thomas. Caring about the struggles his parishioners at Sanford Memorial Church faced, helping them see God's hand at work in their lives, and preaching encouragement and hope from the pulpit of his small church were just what Pastor Jim had in mind when he took the step of faith to enroll in seminary. What he didn't want then—and still doesn't—is the struggle to organize and "administrate" over those in his care. Managing his church overwhelms him daily if he gives it too much thought.

Despite his shepherd's heart, Pastor Jim tried for a while to build his church by using recommended growth principles, but achieving the "200 mark" in membership nearly ruined his home life. The strain left him nothing to give his wife and children. So, he backed off, worked fewer hours, and the inevitable happened. Church attendance slipped to 98.

Now, finances are difficult. Motivation among the flock is lacking. And although he still cares deeply for his people, Reverend Thomas has no idea what to do next.

The Revitalization Curve

As I pointed out in the introduction, most churches in the West are dying—perhaps slowly, *but they are dying.*

Joseph, Hezekiah, Josiah, and Nehemiah faced similarly dire situations. For Joseph, famine would cause the physical deaths of countless people if he didn't take action. Hezekiah faced the challenge of the widespread worship of false gods. Josiah reigned over a kingdom rotting from the inside because of its deviation from God's plan. Nehemiah saw a godly legacy dying unless Jerusalem recovered from its destruction. Each of these leaders needed a way to pour new life into bleak circumstances, much like pastors today.

Churches show a predictable pattern of growth, maturation, and decline that can be depicted by a graph I call the *Lifecycle Curve* or *Bell Curve (see Image 1).* This illustration shows characteristics of a church and the requirements of its leaders at various positions along the curve.

You'll see that the questions about what the church is doing and what it needs to grow are different on the front side of the curve and the back. Knowing these differences is crucial to renewal. For example, if churches don't shift from Visionary Leadership on the front side to Adaptive Leadership on the back side, they simply won't be able to recover their mission.

Every church is somewhere on the Lifecycle Curve, and the sad reality is that *most* churches today are on the back side! Yet, few recognize the need to shift modes of leadership, and even fewer know how to do it.

While vision remains important to effective leadership, you'll notice that leadership on the back side requires a grasp of core values, not just a great vision for what to do next. Churches in decline need to re-capture an understanding of exactly why they exist. What is it that a church is uniquely suited to preserve in the face of society's declining interest in "Christian things"? And sometimes a church needs to *stop* doing things it's been doing—maybe even for years. On the back side of the curve, the organization must change to share the gospel effectively in a new world.

(Image 1)

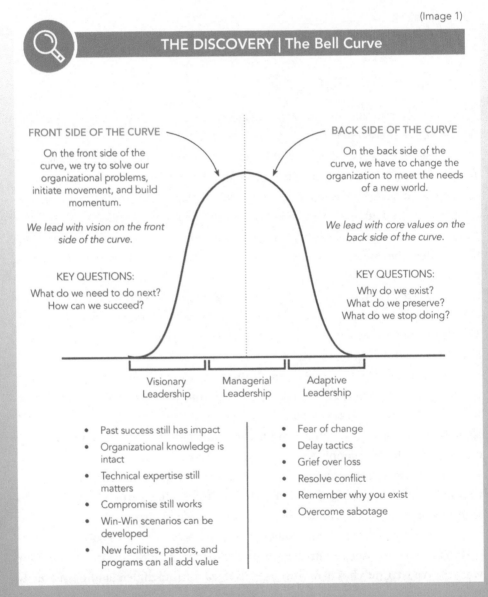

THE DISCOVERY | The Bell Curve

FRONT SIDE OF THE CURVE

On the front side of the curve, we try to solve our organizational problems, initiate movement, and build momentum.

We lead with vision on the front side of the curve.

KEY QUESTIONS:
What do we need to do next?
How can we succeed?

BACK SIDE OF THE CURVE

On the back side of the curve, we have to change the organization to meet the needs of a new world.

We lead with core values on the back side of the curve.

KEY QUESTIONS:
Why do we exist?
What do we preserve?
What do we stop doing?

Visionary Leadership Managerial Leadership Adaptive Leadership

- Past success still has impact
- Organizational knowledge is intact
- Technical expertise still matters
- Compromise still works
- Win-Win scenarios can be developed
- New facilities, pastors, and programs can all add value

- Fear of change
- Delay tactics
- Grief over loss
- Resolve conflict
- Remember why you exist
- Overcome sabotage

Helping you take hold of the "overseer" skills necessary to rescue a church from decline is the goal of this book. In the chapters that follow, we'll look in detail at each step in the challenge, but before we do, a couple of reality checks are needed.

First: How do you know if your church is on the back side of the bell curve?

A quick test is what I call the Trinity of Decline. Churches in decline aren't doing everything wrong. In fact, they are typically doing two out of three extremely important things right. Most declining churches are good at consistent prayer for one another and often feel very close because they are a praying community. They also do well in the corollary attribute of good fellowship. Even declining churches have fostered a community of believers who care for one another.

In a declining church, though, these two positive traits have combined to create an inward-focused culture that leaves a third essential for church health almost completely abandoned. Churches in decline fail miserably at evangelism and outreach. It may be hard to admit that your church is doing a poor job of something as crucial as outreach, but unless you honestly recognize that evangelism just isn't happening, you'll never survive the back side of the bell curve. Churches in decline can usually identify when and how they have "curved in upon themselves" if they will only stop and look.

Second: As valuable as some church growth principles are, they are not adequate for leading churches out of decline on the back side of the curve. Even if you've learned and implemented "church growth principles" in the past, on the back side it's time to shift to principles and skills needed to fulfill the mission necessitated by life in decline. Most church revitalization models will simply reiterate church growth transition models, but this will not only doom the process, it will frustrate those leading it.

Helping you take hold of the "overseer" skills necessary to rescue a church from decline is the goal of this book.

The usual Tuesday morning funk had overtaken Pastor Ken. He opened the bottom drawer of his desk, stuffed in the paper he'd been studying, and slammed the drawer closed. Kenneth Perry squeezed his eyes shut and leaned forward on his desk, hands covering his face.

Maybe Dad was right. I should have been an accountant.

The thought was not a new one. It just cut a little deeper than usual this morning. *What kind of a pastor spends his time creating balance sheets, financial analyses, and organizational charts for his parish?* He glanced down at the drawer in which he'd crammed his most recent profit and loss statement for Gilead Bible Church.

As usual, he felt guilty about so badly wanting to apply the business principles that came naturally to him. His undergraduate years in business school and five years in "the business world" before answering a clear call to ministry had nurtured what now seemed of no consequence to his life's work. He never regretted answering the call—he loved his church and every one of its 527 members. He just didn't feel he had anything left to give them.

The Overseer Role and Why It Is Essential NOW

As the Revitalization Curve shows, survival—and ultimately growing—from the back side requires leadership of a different kind than life on the front side. To that end, here is a modified top-ten list for leading on the back side of the curve that comes from Tod Bolsinger, customized for church revitalization.[1]

1. ***Adaptive leaders cannot reinforce the status quo.***
   Whatever a church is currently doing on the back side of

the curve is not working. Otherwise, it wouldn't be on the back side. Courage to change is essential.

2. ***Adaptive leaders lead internal cultural changes, not just external change.*** Each church develops its own culture, and to make new things happen, changing the culture is required.

3. ***Adaptive leaders will lead by interpreting losses so learning occurs.*** Choosing the right programs, practices, and plans to give up to create necessary change involves a sense of loss among the people. "Grieving" over change, though, can be re-cast by a leader to teach people what benefits are attained as a result. Leading through the grief process is a must.

4. ***Adaptive leaders maintain the necessary stamina for three to seven years of change.*** Back side change doesn't happen overnight. In fact, my hands-on research shows that the initial stages of change usually take at least three years, and it often takes seven for complete transformation to happen. Leading change over the long term is essential.

5. ***Adaptive leaders must unlearn or relearn to successfully navigate change.*** Making change happen begins with the leader. An adaptive leader is open to fresh ideas and new ways of doing things. Learning is required.

6. ***Adaptive leaders identify cognitive dissonance in their followers when they challenge the beliefs their followers have lived by all their lives.*** Back side change inevitably leads people outside of their comfort zones, but a leader must examine carefully the current reality and act accordingly. When the resulting discordant feelings emerge, a competent overseer is ready with

encouragement and reminders of the promise of what's to come.

7. ***Adaptive leaders recognize sabotage and remain steady leaders through this phase of renewal.*** Some folks just won't "get it"—largely because there are a few who simply don't want to. These people create problems a leader must be prepared to address. Sometimes troublemakers even need to be shown the door!

8. ***Adaptive leaders identify the temptation to lose their courage while leading change.*** Leading self is a major requirement for leading others. A strong leader knows he will be tempted to give up in the face of fear or opposition, and he must be inwardly prepared not to.

9. ***Adaptive leaders resist becoming hardened by the battles and challenges they face.*** Tough times come with the territory. Knowing before struggles arrive that the going won't be smooth is part of what allows an adaptive leader to continue. It also helps a leader resist getting angry or bitter over obstacles to growth. Keeping a soft heart within a sturdy exterior is crucial.

10. ***Adaptive leaders don't panic when challenges come.*** They move toward people and embrace the reality of conflict while never surrendering the vision.

Assimilating these characteristics is a tall order for anybody, but it's far from impossible. That's because the skills of a competent overseer provide the template for adopting all of these characteristics.

I've identified six specific skill sets necessary for leading the revitalization of a church. They're so important that I've set up a six-step process suitable for any church wanting to pursue revitalization. Each step engenders one of the skills required of an overseer. This is the process I would walk through with Pastors Bob, Jim, and Ken, and anyone like them to address their differing circumstances (later, I'll explain the names I've given to each set):

SKILL SET #1
Accurately assessing the current situation.
The Discovery

SKILL SET #2
Rightly positioning the church for change.
The Convergence

SKILL SET #3
Clearly casting vision for what can happen.
The Pyramid

SKILL SET #4
Multiplying disciples in the church.
The Path

SKILL SET #5
Rallying other leaders to participate in the plans for change.
The Ladder

SKILL SET #6
Effectively executing the plans crafted for revitalization.
The Toolkit

WHAT IS REFOCUS?

ReFocus is a church revitalization training process that assists pastors with tools to assess their church and restore vibrancy, purpose, and health to their ministry.

Participants will assess the current state of the ministry, consider how to position it for maximum impact, develop all of the directional aspects of ministry, create a custom plan for disciple-making, tailor a leadership development strategy, and build a custom plan for implementation.

THE DISCOVERY	A multi-step approach designed to synthesize data and discoveries, helping pastors to accurately evaluate the current state of the church.
THE CONVERGENCE	A "sweet spot" exercise considering church purpose, leadership passion, and community potential; designed to identify where to position the church's ministry for maximum impact.
THE PYRAMID	An in-depth series of exercises designed to develop all of the directional elements for the church, including mission, strategy, values, vision, annual plan, and goals.
THE PATH	A process that helps develop a customized plan for evangelism and discipleship.
THE LADDER	Creation of a customized, multi-level plan for leadership development, using a four-fold framework (character, competency, chemistry, and concern for the mission).
THE TOOLKIT	Practical resources and ideas to help pastors and church leaders launch the new vision and build momentum toward its fulfillment.

With these overseer skills in place, a church leader readies his flock for renewal, transformation, and the work of revitalization. But how can these same six skill sets work for any church, no matter what the size, location, or stage of decline? It's true that the requirements for revitalization are different for every church. What works for the church down the street may not work for you. That's why the starting point for any productive change is to discover exactly who you really are.

Notes

1. Tod Bolsinger, *Canoeing the Mountains* (Westmont, IL: Intervarsity Press, 2018)

CHAPTER
2

Discover Who You
(and Your Church) Really Are

"We're having problems again with the guy who supplies the coffee lounge."

Lance, the youth pastor at Grace Community Church, glanced self-consciously around the table at Pastor Bob and nine other staff members before continuing.

"I don't mean to sound like I'm complaining or shirking responsibility, but this really doesn't seem like it should be my job. I've got to make plans for the discipleship event for our kids, and solving coffee vendor issues really gets in the way of planning and equipping our leaders."

This really doesn't seem like it should be my job. The words echoed in Bob Dunbar's brain. *How many things don't seem like they should be my job?* He wondered.

Pastor Bob's own distracted thoughts strained his ability to respond sympathetically to his young protégé's concern. Yet, he realized there was truth in the negative observation and managed to disgorge several sentences about the spiritual meaning even of things that didn't seem significant, but he agreed that they would need to think through a better approach so as to keep the youth minister's calling intact.

An hour after the weekly staff meeting concluded, Pastor Bob wandered into a deserted Sunday School classroom. He stood looking at a whiteboard on the wall.

My job?

He cringed at the words. *When did this become just "my job"?*

Ten years ago, he took over this church of 350 members and knew exactly what to do to grow it to today's congregation of nearly ten times that number. He'd won preaching awards in seminary and received mountainous accolades at his first church, so once here, the trajectory was clear: Preach on! Now, though, so many things didn't seem like they should be his job, but they were.

He picked up a dry-erase marker from the tray in front of him and wrote four words on the whiteboard in bright blue ink: Where am I going?

Where Are You Going?

At one time, Pastor Bob knew the answer to the question—at least he assumed that he did. He was going to grow a medium-sized congregation into a big church. The energy behind his assumption, together with his natural gifts, carried him a long way. You might even say he achieved his goal of building a mega-church. Yet, he lost his grip on the answer to the question, "Where are you going?"

The swirl of growth and explosion of challenges that inevitably grew with his church were more than his assumptions and talents could handle. But it brought him back to the right question. Perhaps without even knowing it, he had stumbled into the pattern for healthy leadership change we find in the Bible.

Nehemiah saw the problems of his beloved city, Jerusalem, and even though he had no deserted classroom to retreat to or whiteboard to write on, he did exactly what a spiritual leader should do in his situation. Nehemiah 1:1-4 tells the story:

> *Now it happened in the month Chislev, in the twentieth year, while I was in Susa the capitol, that Hanani, one of my brothers, and some men from Judah came; and I asked them about the Jews who had escaped and had survived the captivity, and about Jerusalem. And they said to me, "The remnant there in the province who survived the captivity are in great distress and disgrace and the wall of Jerusalem is broken down, and its gates have been burned with fire." Now when I heard these words, I sat down and wept and mourned for days, and I was fasting and praying before the God of heaven.*

The simple words "I asked" reveal an incredibly powerful step a good leader will take in difficult circumstances. Nehemiah requests an honest assessment of the situation. Good leaders truly want to know what's up. They don't ignore harsh realities or hide from unpleasant circumstances when it's pertinent to the work they're called to do. Asking can be difficult but is immensely necessary.

When confronted with the reality of Jerusalem's condition, Nehemiah recognized the needs of the city and was not happy about the report. His first action after hearing the news was to humble himself and seek God. He:

◊ **Sat down**—Took a break from other responsibilities to quiet his mind and heart.

◊ **Wept**—Poured out his feelings about the situation.

◊ **Mourned**—Allowed himself to grieve honestly for his home city.

◊ **Fasted**—Realized he would not find the strength within himself to do what is needed and pursued God's help.

◊ **Prayed**—Asked God specifically for direction and intervention on behalf of his desire to take action.

His powerful prayer is recorded in Nehemiah 1:5–11 in which he begs God to intervene. Nehemiah's confession is crucial to his prayer. Not only does he admit to the Jews' culpability for their sin as a nation, he includes himself among the sinners: "*We* have acted very corruptly," he says in verse seven (emphasis mine). Significantly, he doesn't blame others for Jerusalem's problems but rather offers himself as one who has fallen short of deserving God's help.

The importance of personal repentance is difficult to overstate. No matter how well-meaning a church leader may have been, problems that develop in a congregation are—at least to some extent—his fault. "No one's perfect" applies to pastors, and taking responsibility opens the door for God to change and direct toward spiritual renewal.

Wanting an honest assessment of a situation and repenting of wrongdoing takes courage, yet isn't that what we would expect of a spiritual leader? God stands ready to help those who are strong enough to know they need Him. Nehemiah modeled this well. He looked at the dire situation and listened to counsel about what was going on. Perhaps most important, he was open to learning what needed to be done. This attitude is crucial to discovering the direction you should be going.

Pastor Jim breathed a prayer of thanks for his competent church treasurer, one of the most dedicated volunteers at Sanford Memorial. Even though the latest financial report made his stomach churn, at least he knew it was accurate.

Since "working from home" seemed to be the thing to do these days, he had decided to use the kitchen table as his desk. He laid the church's balance sheet next to his coffee cup and shook his head.

Stewardship Sunday was just three weeks away. What would he say to his congregation? Many folks were doing the best they could to give, but there simply wasn't enough to keep the church on solid financial ground. He knew that giving—or not—was a clear measure of a church's well-being. Yet there were other signals his church was in anything but optimal health.

Money problems are obvious. They can't go unnoticed. But fellowship, spiritual vitality? He wasn't sure how to assess those and wondered if anyone really could. Too bad there wasn't a "treasurer" for things like that.

What Is Going on and Why?

At the end of chapter 1, I listed six skill sets necessary for an adaptive leader and mentioned that I would explain the name of each skill set "later." I call the skill set we're discussing in this chapter *The Discovery*. But why?

Discovering exactly who you are and what's going on in your church is the first essential step in knowing where you need to be headed for revitalization to occur. Finding out what's really happening requires an ability to accurately assess your situation. You must drill down in every area of church life and get to the heart of issues to bring new vitality to your congregation.

When I consult with churches, the process for analyzing the health of a church often seems like a mystery to a pastor, staff, and lay leaders—at least at first. Like Jim Thomas, the situation is so overwhelming they have no idea where to start. That's when the power of *The Discovery* skill set and steps for church assessment become obvious. It's important to look both at what is happening in your church right now as well as to review your church's history.

Understanding Your Church's NOW

There is a matrix of ten discernible points on which to assess the health of a church. As I begin talking with leaders about their church, a few of the points become obvious—worship, evangelism, discipleship, and stewardship—but some are much less so. For instance, what hospitality does your church offer visitors? How is organizational structure helping or hurting your ministry? I've outlined below each of the ten points of overall church health as described in Acts 2:42–47. I further suggest several of the many items that typically need to be assessed regarding each point.

1. **HOSPITALITY**—Determine whether or not your facilities are able to support the vision of your church. To do this, you'll want to consider what coming to your church is like for a visitor. Is the building's appearance inviting? Is parking convenient? Do you have signage outside and inside that eases the stress of finding the way around? Do you have greeters for every service? Are your facilities and services designed to accommodate visitors of all ages? How quickly do you follow up with newcomers?

2. **WORSHIP**—Evaluate the degree to which worship draws people further into relationship with God. Is it inspiring to unchurched as well as those who attend every week? Does the music help people connect with God? Are the services well-planned, and do the worship leaders "debrief" so as to continuously improve? Do sermons speak to the life situations of your hearers?

3. **EVANGELISM**—Reaching your community for Christ lies at the core of a church's mission, so you need to understand how well you're doing in this key element of church life. Are your church membership classes set up to determine where participants are spiritually, and are you training members how to share their faith? How many of your visitors become baptized followers of Christ? Does your church look for creative ways to share the gospel and speak in culturally-relevant ways to non-believers?

4. **DISCIPLESHIP**—You want your congregation to grow in Christ and need to know how well that is working. Do you see lives transformed, and does your church provide a clear pathway for spiritual growth? Is your small group ministry effective at making disciples? Do people have easy ways to connect with a group? Do you add groups as needed to

stimulate growth? Is there a plan in place to nurture group leaders and to "disciple your disciple-makers"?

5. **SERVICE**—Active service to the church by its members is a key determinant of a church's health and well-being. Do your members have a vision for using their gifts to serve others within the congregation and go about their service with joy? Is there a sense among your people that they grow spiritually by serving and that God uses their service to accomplish His work? What proportion of your members actively serve? Do your members feel free to minister in the community in the name of your church?

6. **FELLOWSHIP**—Joyful interaction among Christians is a delight to any congregation, and fostering such an environment is critical. Do your people visibly enjoy being together (laughter, smiles, upbeat conversations)? Is the environment encouraging, and are conflicts resolved easily and quickly? Are people experiencing a common sense of purpose and on the lookout to meet each other's needs? Do your leaders let people know their contributions are appreciated, and can members discuss their personal problems without fearing they will become a target of gossip?

7. **PRAYER**—Seeking God's heart for a church is essential. Do church members regularly pray for one another and celebrate answers? Does the church look to God for guidance in bringing people to Christ, in missions outreach, and for the resources needed for ministry? Are leaders modeling what it means to walk closely with the Lord, and are daily Bible reading and prayer encouraged in the lives of members? Are members praying for the leaders?

8. **STEWARDSHIP**—Finances reflect the spiritual condition of a church and are a material requirement for growth and revitalization. Are you actively developing members from first-time givers to generous givers who offer tithes and more? Do you provide regular messages about the blessing of giving? How successful was your last financial stewardship campaign, and does your church typically meet or exceed its income budget? Do people tend to give unrestricted gifts as opposed to those designated for specific ministries or projects?

9. **LEADERSHIP**—A church will not grow past its leadership, so cultivating resilient leaders is essential. Do church leaders serve with joy, and do members follow enthusiastically? Are leaders in a position to utilize their gifts, and do they receive training to further their abilities? Do your leaders have a clear understanding of the vision and direction of your church? Are you organized to facilitate accomplishing your mission, strategy, and values? Are lay people held accountable for the work they have volunteered to do?

10. **ORGANIZATIONAL STRUCTURE**—The way you're set up determines what you will accomplish. Does your church have a system in place for creating annual goals and the structure to meet them? Do volunteers know why their work is important? Does the organizational structure support your vision, and do the ministries of your church understand how they work together to accomplish the goals of your church? Do leaders meet regularly to assess church ministries, and are activities well planned? Does the congregation know what the goals of your church are?

Asking these questions of yourself and other church leaders is the critical first step in discovering where your church is right now and in getting ready to make other assessments about where to go next.

Below, you will find a sample scoring of the *Church Health Survey* (*Image 2*).

(Image 2)

THE DISCOVERY | Church Health Survey

EXAMPLE

Compile your score for each section as well as the scores of everyone else on your team in the table below:

PARTICIPANT NAME	Bob	Robin	Fred	Carol	Madison						AVERAGE
First Impressions	63	61	71	84	65						69
Worship	77	71	77	91	40						71
Evangelism	66	67	64	80	31						62
Discipleship	67	54	57	86	31						59
Service	64	52	66	67	44						59
Fellowship	72	67	78	81	51						70
Prayer	80	79	91	84	58						78
Stewardship	63	63	37	80	60						61
Leadership	63	80	37	91	42						63
Organizational Structure	64	69	62	66	32						59

Understanding Your Church's PAST

Knowing where you've come from sheds much-needed light on what your church is going through right now, and it also lays useful groundwork in deciding where to go from here. In working with churches, I've uncovered some remarkable secrets of grasping the meaning of your church's past and its impact on the future.

Studying what I call *Historic Trends* is vital. There are five aspects of church life you need to reflect on to grasp what trends are working for or against you: baptisms, worship attendance, small group attendance, new membership, and overall membership. The best way I've found to analyze the impact of each of these is simply to plot them on a graph. If you want to know how you're doing with baptisms in your church, you can set up a graph that looks something like *Image 3*.

(Image 3)

THE DISCOVERY | Historic Trends: Normative-size Church

EXAMPLE

BAPTISMS & NEW MEMBERSHIP

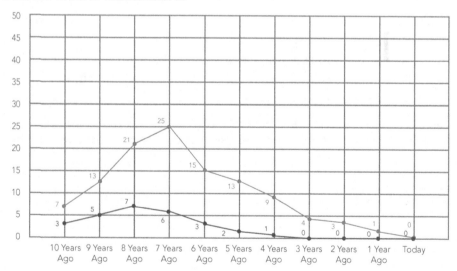

The above example shows a church that had 25 baptisms per year seven years ago, 15 six years ago, 13 five years ago, 9 four years ago, 4 three years ago, 3 two years ago,

27

1 one year ago, and zero so far this year. As you can see, this suggests a downward trend in baptisms—clearly a signal to be factored into the assessment of the church's condition.

Seeing a "picture" like this of your situation is eye-opening, and this same process can show what's going on in the other four critical aspects of historic church life. To do that, you'll need to substitute figures on the y-axis (vertical) that suit the range for your numbers of worship attendance, small group attendance, new membership, and overall membership.

In addition to charting your *Historic Trends*, it is valuable to reflect on positive and not-so-positive (I prefer to call them "challenging") church experiences. These would be circumstances, events, conflicts, or the like that manifested themselves during the life of your church—whether you're five years old or 200 years old. I generally recommend that leaders brainstorm a list of 10–25 events like this and list them in two columns—one positive and one challenging. Then, select the five most significant from each and graph them.

I call this the *Ebb & Flow* exercise. After deciding on your top five situations in each category, they can be plotted on another graph like that shown in *Image 4*.

In the sample church's 40-year graph, the five positive experiences are plotted (P1, P2, P3, etc.) above the line in the years in which each occurred, along with an estimate, on a scale of zero to ten, of how of positive the experiences were. Similarly, the challenging experiences are plotted below the 40-year line (C1, C2, etc.).

The plotted points reveal two different characteristics of your church. The positive experiences reveal your passions, and the challenging ones reveal your character development. Experiences seem "positive" because they tap into the things your church is passionate about. Conversely, experiences "challenge" a church at points where it needs to grow stronger or more faithful.

(Image 4)

THE DISCOVERY | Ebb & Flow

EXAMPLE

Part two of the *Ebb & Flow* exercise consists of charting these experiences over time. In order to chart the events, you must first create your time line. If your church is 200 years old, you will want each mark to represent 20 years. If your church is five years old, you will want each mark to represent a three-month period of time. You can adjust the time line to fit your church's history. Then determine how positive the event was by grading the experience from +10 to -10.

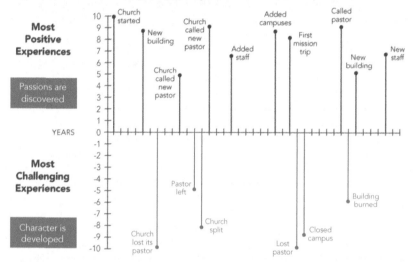

Look carefully at the ebb and flow of the church across time. What patterns can you discern? What discoveries did you make? Remember that the more positive the experience, the deeper a passion it may be. Conversely, the more negative the experience, the deeper the character development will run.

⬤ EBB & FLOW SUMMARY

Reflect on both *Ebb & Flow* exercises and identify your discoveries.

1. *The church is in a cycle of highs and lows based on their pastors.*
2. *The church must become more stable during pastoral transitions.*
3. *New significant ministries have a big impact on the church.*
4. *The mission of the church must become more important than people and facilities.*
5. _____

| Based on the trends identified in the **Ebb & Flow Summary**, how serious is the need for the church to refocus? | ☐ Strategic | ☐ Immediate |
| | ☐ Necessary | ☐ Urgent |

"It seems to me you've made a basic assumption that may not be valid."

"I'm not sure what you mean." Ken Perry studied his dad's face across the restaurant table. Monthly lunches with his favorite and longest-known mentor was one of the brightest spots in his schedule.

"Your gifts. Your business school studies. Your natural inclinations for accounting and organizational problems. I meant that, ever since you attended seminary, you seem to have decided they have no place in your life. Believe me, I'm as proud as any father could be of what you've accomplished in your ministry at Gilead Bible Church, but it worries me to think you've abandoned an important—and dare I say it?—God-given part of your life."

Pastor Ken dropped his eyes to the half-eaten sandwich on his plate. The two men sat in silence for nearly a minute before the hint of a smile began to form on Ken's face. He looked up at his dad.

"That's amazing. I've assumed the worst about my love of business and numbers and never have really considered the possibility that there's a place for them in my ministry." He let out a deep breath, then continued. "I've felt at such a loss this past year to know where I'm headed, let alone where I should be taking the congregation. But maybe somehow you've given me a key to finding out. I'm not sure how, but it's worth exploring."

Discovery Gets the Church's Attention and Creates a Spiritual Burden

Regardless of how positive or challenging the observations are in *The Discovery*, the good news is that unearthing a real picture of your situation always gets people's attention.

Even more, for those committed to Christ and your church, it creates a healthy, spiritual desire to make changes.

To round out your *Discovery* process, three particular aspects of church life need to be evaluated: The overall *spiritual* health of your congregation, the vitality of your church's *ministry*, and the *systems* set up within your church to accomplish its vision. These drill down into the core elements of church life and deepen the understanding you gained from the ten points we reviewed about church health.

When I consult with churches on spiritual, ministry, and systems assessments, I work through a detailed list of issues and rate them so as to create an in-depth picture of church life. To wrap up this *Discovery* chapter, I'll walk you through an overview of the issues and what you should look for in each category as you do your own analysis.

Spiritual Assessment

The spiritual maturity of a church says a lot about the starting point for making changes. A church lacking in maturity needs help in spiritual growth as part of your revitalization plan while a more mature church will show the spiritual resources you have to work with to make needed changes.

A variety of factors come into play when you assess spiritual maturity. Here are some of the key points to consider:

◇ Grounding in doctrine

◇ Participation by the people in mission work beyond the congregation

◇ Degree to which members share their faith regularly with outsiders

◇ Quality and intensity of congregational and personal prayer life

◇ Meeting each other's needs and taking joy in fellowship

◇ The church's ability to meet its financial obligations

Once you've honestly considered where you are as a whole in spiritual maturity, you need to take a hard look at ministry within the church.

Ministry Assessment

Your ministry assessment not only looks at what you're doing now, but it is also where you begin to think about how your church and its leaders may react to the changes needed for revitalization. You'll want to set aside time from your typical routine to ruminate on where you stand. These are some of the questions that will help your thinking:

◇ How clear is your current vision to the congregation, and how well are you moving forward together?

◇ How well do you think the existing church culture will embrace a new vision, and how effective do you believe the church staff and lay leadership can be in leading the church to accept it?

◇ Are your members aware that a vision is necessary? If not very aware, will they appreciate having a clear vision?

◇ Is the church membership mobilized for service in all areas of missions: local, national, and global?

◇ Do the events on your church calendar support the mission of the church?

◇ Does your church budget support the work of evangelism and discipleship?

System Assessment

Whether you've spent a lot of time setting up operating systems for your church or not, there are systems in place. Somehow, the church does what the church does, even if it has not thought it through. The degree to which your systems are well thought out and effectively implemented, though, determines a lot about whether or not you accomplish what matters most to you and your congregation. Here are some of the major questions you'll want to consider:

◇ Do you have a process in place to incorporate visitors into the membership of your church?

◇ Are your existing facilities able to support a different or growing ministry?

◇ Does the church's vision drive the budgeting process, and are you actively developing the stewardship of your members?

◇ Do you have adequate staff, and is the staff structure built around the strategy of your church?

◇ Is communication within your church effective in letting members know about activities, ministry opportunities, and even the vision itself?

◇ How strong is your small group organization?

◇ Do you have a training plan for evangelism, discipleship, and equipping for service?

The Message in Your Discovery

You'll recall from chapter 1 that every church is somewhere on the Revitalization Curve, which indicates what sort of leadership challenges a church faces. *Discovery* begins to put together the picture you'll need to address the issues inherent to your place on the Curve.

Assembling a clear image of your church's state of being should open your eyes—and that of your congregation—to the good and not-so-good aspects of your current church life. Just as the four gospels, taken together, offer perspective to give a complete picture of who Jesus is, so this multi-faceted assessment provides the courageous pastor a full and complete portrait of his church's current reality. Because so many factors are considered, this picture goes beyond what numbers alone might show. The assessment is also narrative. Together, these components provide a numeric, spiritual, ministry, and mission assessment that outlines the greatest opportunities and challenges for the church.

From this evaluation, you can be encouraged by the things that are working well, and you might take a deep breath over the things that aren't. For both, though, the message that emerges begins to point a direction for renewal.

As with Nehemiah, the spiritual "burden" this places on the hearts of your people can become a wonderful motivator for moving ahead in the work of revitalization. In the next step, you'll get to see exactly what opportunities emerge from what you know about yourself and your church.

———————————

For Deeper Discovery

In my closing comments, I mention the value a "courageous pastor" will derive from pursuing all angles of *Discovery*. You can benefit by digging deeper and taking the three bold steps I suggest below.

1. ***Tell your story.*** Write out the most honest narrative you can muster about where your church has come from and what that means about where you are now.

2. ***Interview your members.*** Ask a selection of your congregation members to tell you their version of your church's story. In one particularly poignant example I ran into one time, a Sunday School teacher asked her fourth graders to write down the story of the church from their perspective. When the pastor read the kids' insights, he was astounded by what he learned by looking through their eyes.

3. ***Ask "safe" questions of key people.*** One pastor I know of wrote four questions to discuss with his men's discipleship group that allowed them to share openly their thoughts about the church.

3

Convergence:
Your Church's "Sweet Spot"

Pastor Bob Dunbar scrolled through the summaries of the transcripts from the latest round of membership questionnaires. Randomly, he paused, allowing himself to read some of the comments from the people who sat in the pews before him and watched him online each Sunday.

"We love being at Grace Community Church, but it took months for us to really feel like we fit in at such a big place."

"I feel inspired and energized after the pastor's sermons, but I'm not sure what to do about it, once I leave the service."

"I wish I knew better ways to get my unchurched friends here."

"We've thought about starting a ministry for underprivileged single moms, but it's hard to get anybody else interested."

"I've been teaching in the fifth grade Sunday School for five years straight, and I can't remember the last time anybody said, 'thank you.'"

Some of the comments made him wince, but Bob made himself keep reading. After all, he was the one who had called together the advisory team to reach out widely to the membership. He had told them to ask questions, listen closely to the answers, and record them just as they came from the lips of church members; "I want to read it exactly the way they say it," he had instructed them. But as he read the comments, he felt the challenge, deep in his heart, of bringing together all the diversity of the church in a way that could reposition it for the future. His seminary days were long past, but he knew that nothing in his training there had prepared him with the skill set he needed to help this church get back on the path to a meaningful, relevant future.

Driven by an increasing sense of frustration and the feeling that he was pouring from a rapidly emptying jug, Bob had resolved to learn, with the deepest focus he could bring to the task, what was going on in the minds and hearts of the people to whom God had called him to minister. The advisory team—and these messages from his congregation—were the start toward some answers. At least, he hoped so.

As Bob read, it became clearer and clearer why his secretary had to screen so many requests for meetings with his congregants; the people in the pews of his church had myriad needs, each highly individualized and specific. But they also had dreams for the church, for what it could be, and that realization, despite feeling like an impossible challenge, also gave Bob a strange sense of hope. For so long he had assumed that *his* vision was driving the church's health and growth, but learning that the people in the pews had dreams and hopes for the church made him understand that something—or rather, Someone—greater than himself was at work in the lives of this church. He gave a rueful smile and shook his head. *After this many years as a pastor*, he thought, *it turns out I was the one who needed to be reminded of Who is really in charge, Who is positioning this church to fulfill its mission in the world.*

Bob refocused on his computer screen and continued reading. He had a feeling that some important themes were emerging from the comments of his flock, and he prayed that the Holy Spirit would guide him to perceive them…

"I Know You": Christ's Call to Convergence

While walking the dusty streets of Jerusalem with his disciples, Jesus taught one of the most important principles of spiritual leadership when he said these words: "… He calls his own sheep by name and leads them out. When he has brought out all his own, he goes ahead of them, and his sheep follow him, for they know his voice" (John 10:3,4).

No one knows the church—the wants, needs, dreams, desires, and hurts of each of its people—as well as the Great Overseer who is constantly watching over those whom he loves. As fellow pastors under the authority of the great "Overseer of our souls" (1 Peter 2:25, ESV), we need look no further than his very own words to learn what we must do to call the church under our care—and ourselves—to rejoin our Lord on the path of renewed, reinvigorated focus on the mission of Christ's church in the world. By turning to the words of the risen Christ in Revelation, chapters 2 and 3, we can gain a better understanding of how the Overseer himself calls to his people and invites them to follow.

> To the angel of the church in Ephesus, write:
> The One who holds the seven stars in his right hand, the One who walks among the seven golden lampstands, says this: "I know your deeds, and your labor and perseverance, and that you cannot tolerate evil people, and you have put those who call themselves apostles to the test, and they are not, and you found them to be false; and you have perseverance and have endured on account of My name, and have not become weary. But I have this against you that you have left your first love. Therefore, remember from where you have fallen, and repent, and do the deeds you did at first; or else I am coming to you and I will remove your lampstand from its place…."

And to the angel of the church in Smyrna, write:
The first and the last, who was dead and has come to life, says
this: "I know your tribulation and your poverty (but you are
rich) and the slander of those who say they are Jews and are
not, but are a synagogue of Satan.... Be faithful until death,
and I will give you the crown of life...." (Revelation 2:1–10).

When we read the risen Christ's words to each of the seven churches of Asia as relayed by the Apostle John, a striking pattern emerges. At the beginning of each admonition to a particular church, Jesus' first two words are, "I know..." Perhaps we shouldn't be surprised, but consider closely what Christ is doing in each of these "mini-sermons" to the seven churches. Out of his perfect knowledge of who, what, and where they are, including all the past events and circumstances that have brought them to the present moment, the Lord is providing a simple, clear, powerful word that can energize and refocus each church on its original mission, purpose, and passion. Jesus knew that the church would need constant renewal until his eventual return; in fact, his last recorded words in scripture are aimed at this very purpose!

As he speaks to the seven churches out of his perfect knowledge, Jesus gives them a single focus, an empowering idea that will guide them to the "sweet spot" where their ministry can be uniquely positioned; where their strengths can be leveraged together; and where they can fully utilize all the resources and opportunities God has given them. In short, Jesus is directing the churches to their point of *convergence*: the place where their leaders' passions and the churches' purpose, community, and potential intersect with the next step of faith God desires.[1]

Getting to the Church's "Big Idea"

Notice the counsel given to the churches:

◊ The church in Ephesus was told to refocus on their *love* (Revelation 2:1–7);

◊ The church in Smyrna was told to refocus on their *faith* and their *hope* (Revelation 2:8–11);

◇ The church in Pergamum was told to refocus on their *teaching* (Revelation 2:12–17);

◇ The church in Thyatira was told to refocus on their *works* (Revelation 2:18–29);

◇ The church in Sardis was told to refocus on their *purity* (Revelation 3:1–6);

◇ The church in Philadelphia was told to refocus on their *opportunity* (Revelation 3:7–13);

◇ The church in Laodicea was told to refocus on their *priorities* (Revelation 3:14–22).

Take a moment to consider each of these in turn. Two of them seem particularly pertinent to the concept of convergence in the church. First, let's take a look at Ephesus. Just think of the great tradition of teaching, ministry, and doctrine this church had inherited. None less than the great Apostle Paul himself had laid the foundations for the church at Ephesus, and these Christians were the recipients of one of the most profound treatises in the Bible; John Calvin called the Letter to the Ephesians "the queen of the epistles." Even today, we still marvel when we read this epistle and its inspired treatment of the great themes of the unity of the Body of Christ, the ordering of the Christian household, God's power for the believer's daily life in the world, and all the other deeply influential teachings presented by Paul.

And yet, despite the weighty traditions of teaching and sound doctrine from its very beginnings, the church at Ephesus still needed to be reminded and refocused on one of the most foundational Christian principles: love. Even though the founder of the church, the Apostle Paul, presents in 1 Corinthians 13 his beautiful treatise on love as the "greatest of these" and had doubtless spent hours planting this teaching in the hearts and minds of his hearers in Ephesus, his spiritual children had, in only a single generation, forgotten this fundamental principle. This should encourage us to remember that no matter how big, how well-known, or how influential a church gets, it can never outgrow the need for renewal and refocus. As pastors, our task is to breathe in deeply the Word of God, to discern the leading of the Holy Spirit for the body of believers, and to continually reset our course in the same direction. Indeed, as the great pastor John Stott once said to me, "The church is always in need of renewal, and pastors must lead the work of constantly renewing the church."

Now let's think about the church in Philadelphia. Notice that Christ offers no critique at all of this body of believers. Instead, he points to their patient endurance and faithfulness despite the opposition they are suffering that has sapped their strength. And then he tells them, "I have placed before you an open door that no one can shut." Despite their obstacles and what seems to be their failing strength, Jesus asks them to refocus on the open door. Wouldn't it be amazing if each of our churches could be called "the church of the open door"? And isn't it heartening to know that even when we feel our own strength failing, the power of the risen Lord is opening a door for us to reposition the church so that it can be more fully engaged in its mission?

The point is, when a church reflects upon its purpose, its leaders' passions, and its community potential, it will discover its convergence point. Jesus used this very pattern seven times to renew and revitalize seven churches, and we can confidently follow Christ's pattern with the same effect. In fact, following it is essential for churches who wish to remain relevant and engaged in the mission the Lord has for them in the world.

Far too many churches don't realize that this need even exists or stop to consider how they can learn where and how Jesus wants to reposition them. Instead, they borrow an idea from somewhere else or develop a catchy or creative approach that may be based on the latest buzzword or corporate management principle *du jour*. Most have never considered that Christ already has a principle that has been in place for over 2,000 years—a process driven by the Holy Spirit that will develop the repositioning point where churches are led to discern their place of convergence.

This is the crux of *The Convergence* process. When an overseer, working under the authority of the Great Overseer, leads a church to truly engage with it, they are able to discover their "big idea": the empowering, succinct word from the Holy Spirit that informs and empowers their renewed mission and purpose.

Pastor Jim put down the pencil, took a final look at the budget spreadsheet, and stood up. He walked to the window in his office and stared outside. He knew he needed to finish going over the budget reports, but the comments and discussion from last night's committee meeting kept running on a loop through his mind.

Esther Callan, one of the oldest members of Sanford Memorial, had addressed the entire group at one point. Her voice thin with age, she nevertheless fairly vibrated with conviction when she said, "I remember the bad days, after the war, when so many of the young men of this church who went away to fight never came home. Families here were hurting. I could hear it in the voices of my own parents. But one thing I never heard from anyone was whether this church would minister to our community. This was always a church that understood the problems of the people in our neighborhoods. We adjusted to the needs. We cared for people and helped them follow Jesus. And I believe this church can still be a place like that. We just need to know where the problems are."

Jim smiled at the memory. The temperature in the room seemed to change as Esther spoke. It was as if this stooped, 80-something-year-old woman had reminded every person on the committee of something they'd known all along, but had forgotten.

Mining the memories, perceptions, and beliefs of the members of the church had been a deeply revealing exercise—not all of it pleasant. But the undercurrent beneath much of what Jim's review had uncovered had convinced him that at a fundamental level, most of his parishioners felt a strong commitment toward obeying the call of Christ to fulfill the mission of the church. Not only that, they expressed a commitment to becoming better stewards of the mission God had given them.

For the first time in a long time, Pastor Thomas was sensing that his flock had a deep desire to be led *toward* something. The questions his people were asking themselves—and more importantly, the answers they were getting—whispered to him that the Holy Spirit was ready to move. As pastor, he just needed wisdom to know where to reposition the church for the future.

The Power of Convergence

As we seek to guide our churches toward the point of convergence, remember that the ultimate goal is to unleash the unique gifts, open doors of opportunity in the community, and give free rein to the leadership passions that God has placed in the church to carry out his mission in the world. As pastors, we must believe confidently that the Great Overseer will never ask us to do anything without also provisioning us and those we lead for the tasks to which we are called. Will there be challenges? Yes, and usually the challenges come from within; our resistance to change, our lack of faith, and our desire to make people happy will create obstacles that must be overcome. But the mission of God is too important for God's people to be distracted by these lesser things.

What Would Jesus Say?

One way to think about the impact and importance of the convergence in our churches is to consider the question, "What would Jesus say to our church if He gave us a word, similar to those in Revelation 2 and 3?" Might He direct our attention to a ministry need in our community that is going unmet? Would He show us a group of people whom He loves but who are being ignored by the rest of the community? Would He call us to re-examine our financial priorities so that the work of the church might be better provisioned? Would He say, "I see you worshipping on Sunday morning, but I do not see you serving the world on Monday morning"? What would He affirm? What would He single out for challenge or correction?

The fact is, of course, that Jesus *is* visiting our churches—every moment of every day. He is casting his eyes over His flock and urging us, through the prompting of the Holy Spirit, to come and follow. He is speaking into the hearts of those He has appointed as pastors, prompting them to exercise the ministry of spiritual leadership. He is, in other words, constantly calling His church to reposition itself in a place to fulfill its mission. This is the church's convergent point.

Because we do not have the benefit of the risen Christ's divine and perfect knowledge, we must commit to spending the time needed—and enduring the inevitable discomfort—in answering important questions and having challenging discussions with the significant leaders in the church. This will unearth certain hopes, dreams, fears, challenges, perceptions, and beliefs of the people in the pews.

The next step in the process, then, is to focus on the place where those aspirations, abilities, and beliefs all come together. That is where God will call upon His people to step out in faith as they begin to consider the direction of the mission the Lord will give to the church.

The "What" behind the "Why"

With all your discoveries fresh on your mind, you will next want to begin to think about the church's *purpose*, the leaders' *passions*, and the community's *potential*. This triad of concepts has offered a tried-and-true method for positioning businesses in the marketplace and has been validated over and over since it was first introduced by Jim Collins in his book, *Good to Great*. But what most people don't realize is that this model has actually been around a lot longer than Jim Collins! In fact, it has been around since Jesus announced it at the end of the first century, applying it to seven churches to help them reposition for renewal and revitalization. The aim of *The Convergence* is to position the church at the intersection of its purpose, the leaders' passion, and the community's potential. Here is how you do it:

1. **CHURCH'S PURPOSE**—The church's purpose answers the questions: Why does your church exist? What is most important to the congregation? Honing and clarifying purpose is the most important step in differentiating your church from all the other organizations in the community.

2. **LEADERS' PASSION**—Another key to discovering the church's convergence is to discover what the church's leadership is passionate about. When the church leadership has a relentless passion that is unleashed, it can realize its

full ministry potential. It's vital to ask: What skills does the church's leadership exhibit? What does leadership get most excited about? What do others say you are good at?

3. **POTENTIAL**—The final piece of this puzzle is to consider the community's potential. You should ask questions like: What is your community's greatest need? What problem can the church solve? What is your community known for? Answering these questions will help you evaluate where the church can step in with the Gospel and make a difference for Jesus in the lives of the people who live around the church.

Once all of these considerations are taken into account, the principal work is done and only one step remains to determine your convergence. We call this developing your "big idea." This will require you to step out in faith and consider what is next for the church. The "big idea"—equivalent to the word Jesus gave to each of the seven churches—becomes the defining direction for the mission statement and other vision elements for the church.

Thinking in the Presence of God

The principal method in *The Convergence* process is to pose a series of thoughtful questions to a group of leaders in the church and then listen closely, in a Holy Spirit–empowered way, to the discussion. The goal, of course, is to arrive at a greater understanding of God's vision for the church, along with the resources He is providing for the realization of the vision.

Questions for uncovering community *potential* might include:

1. What is our community's greatest challenge?

2. What problem is no one addressing in our community?

3. What part of our community's life is the farthest from God's original design?

4. What is our community known for?

5. What is the historical background and narrative of our community?

6. What is the one change that, if it happened, would make the greatest difference in our community?

Questions for considering your church's *purpose* might look something like this:

1. What does our church believe its mission to be?

2. What is most important to our church?

3. If our church had to do only one thing, what would it be?

4. What one practice or activity would cause the most trouble for our pastor if it were discontinued?

5. What verses from the Bible most clearly define our church's purpose?

6. What does our church unify around most readily?

Questions to help you think about your church's leadership *passion* might be like the following:

1. What special skills, talents, or abilities does our leadership exhibit?

2. What aspect of ministry is our leadership most passionate about?

3. What topic in ministry does our leadership read about, attend conferences for, or discuss with other pastors the most?

4. What aspect of ministry does our leadership team enjoy discussing the most?

5. What does our leadership believe the church finds easiest to do?

6. What do other churches say our church is good at?

Keep in mind that there is no single correct answer or set of answers for these questions. Rather, they are intended to encourage church members, pastors, and other leaders to "think in the presence of God" about who the church is, what its aspirations are, and where God may be leading the body of believers.

Depending on your church's history, traditions, position in the community, and other variables, the convergence conversation will uncover various themes that can then be placed in a matrix, a "pyramid" that you can use to guide yourself and your church to *The Convergence* "sweet spot": the "big idea" that best blends the church's vision, aspirations, abilities, and positioning for ministry in the community.

Careful, prayerful contemplation of these themes will then lead to the apex, or top of the pyramid: the principal ideas that capture and distill the next step of faith and obedience. This should represent the convergence of the church's purpose, the leadership's passion, and the community's potential. Ideally, the *Convergence* process will culminate with the emergence of two summarizing words: one key action word and a second, descriptive word that brings into focus the mission and goal. It may even be a short phrase, but this "big idea" will be used to inform and develop the church's mission statement, strategy, and vision.

A completed *Sweet Spot Pyramid* might resemble the example in *Image 5*.

By now, you will have probably realized that the engine powering this process is knowledge, fueled by conviction. Remember, each of Jesus' messages to the seven churches of Asia started with the words, "I know." By leading your church through the discovery and convergence processes, you—and they—will have gained a tremendous amount of knowledge about your church: its past, its faith roots, its place in the community, its leaders, its hopes and dreams. By asking probing questions and listening to the answers under the influence of God's Holy Spirit, you will be able to name and clearly visualize the empowering idea that will lead the church toward its next great step of faith, the first and most important step in the journey toward realizing God's greater purpose for his church.

What would Jesus say to your church? Discovering the answer through *The Convergence process* will position your church to achieve what Christ urged, over and over again, in Revelation 2 and 3: "Whoever has ears, let them hear what the Spirit says to the churches."

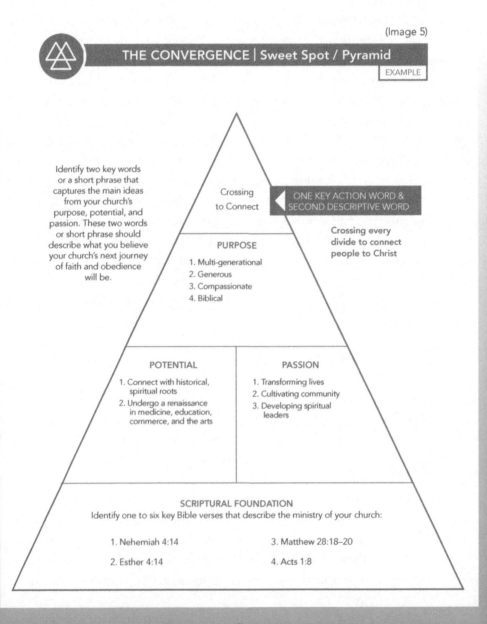

(Image 5)

THE CONVERGENCE | Sweet Spot / Pyramid

EXAMPLE

Identify two key words or a short phrase that captures the main ideas from your church's purpose, potential, and passion. These two words or short phrase should describe what you believe your church's next journey of faith and obedience will be.

Crossing to Connect

ONE KEY ACTION WORD & SECOND DESCRIPTIVE WORD

Crossing every divide to connect people to Christ

PURPOSE

1. Multi-generational
2. Generous
3. Compassionate
4. Biblical

POTENTIAL

1. Connect with historical, spiritual roots
2. Undergo a renaissance in medicine, education, commerce, and the arts

PASSION

1. Transforming lives
2. Cultivating community
3. Developing spiritual leaders

SCRIPTURAL FOUNDATION
Identify one to six key Bible verses that describe the ministry of your church:

1. Nehemiah 4:14
2. Esther 4:14
3. Matthew 28:18–20
4. Acts 1:8

Notes

1. These principles were first outlined in Jim Collins, *Good to Great: Why Some Companies Make the Leap... and Others Don't* (Harper Business, 2001) and later refined for churches by Thom S. Rainer in *Breakout Churches: Discover How to Make the Leap* (Zondervan, 2005).

PART 2

Gain Wisdom for God's Direction

CHAPTER
4

The Blessing of Mission, Values, and Strategy

Pastor Ken Perry took a moment to look at each of the other faces around the conference table. He wondered if the timing was right for what he was about to say.

Charles Clemons returned his gaze steadily, his dark eyes unblinking. Charles had built a successful auto repair business and was a leader in the community as well as at Gilead Bible Church. He had a huge heart for reaching the lost, as anyone would learn by talking with him for more than five minutes.

Seated next to Charles was Margie Roberson. Margie was the city's most prominent financial planner; she was also Ken's principal encourager. Since the day Ken had accepted the call to the church, he had felt a special kinship with Margie—probably because they shared an innate understanding and appreciation for business, finance, and the stories numbers could tell.

He looked at the rest of them: all good, caring people, faithful in attendance at church, involved in the community. But were they ready for the vision he was about to cast?

All authority has been given to me ... The words fell into Ken's mind unbidden—and yet, he realized they had been in his heart since this meeting had started. *Go, therefore...* Ken knew that this was the moment God had been preparing. It was time to speak...

The Interplay of Mission, Values, and Strategy

Earlier, we considered the call God placed upon Nehemiah, an expatriate Jew who occupied a position of influence in the court of the Persian emperor Artaxerxes. When he asked about the condition of Jerusalem and his fellow countrymen who still lived nearby, he learned of their distress and the desolation of the city. Nehemiah took the first step that any good leader should take: he asked the right questions and listened carefully to the answers. And even though what he learned was deeply upsetting, he did not look away. Instead, he allowed himself to grieve over the condition of God's people; he fasted and prayed, knowing that only through the strength provided by God could he do what needed to be done; and most important of all, he accepted personal responsibility for both the great need of his homeland and the steps necessary to resolve the difficulty.

In Nehemiah chapter 2, we find the gripping account of what happens next.

> And it came about in the month Nisan, in the twentieth year of King Artaxerxes, that wine was before him, and I picked up the wine and gave it to the king. Now I had not been sad in his presence, so the king said to me, "Why is your face sad, though you are not ill? This is nothing but sadness of heart." Then I was very much afraid. And I said to the king, "May the king live forever. Why should not my face be sad, when the city, the site of my fathers' tombs, is desolate and its gates have been consumed by fire?" Then the king said to me, "What would you request?" So I prayed to the God of heaven. Then I said to the king, "If it pleases the king, and if your servant has found favor before you, I request that you send me to Judah, to the city of my fathers' tombs, that I may rebuild it."

Then the king said to me, with the queen sitting beside him, "How long will your journey be, and then will you return?" So it pleased the king to send me, and I gave him a definite time. And I said to the king, "If it pleases the king, let letters be given me for the governors of the provinces beyond the River, so that they will allow me to pass through until I come to Judah, and a letter to Asaph, the keeper of the king's forest, that he will give me timber to make beams for the gates of the citadel which is by the temple, for the wall of the city, and for the house to which I will go." And the king granted them to me because the good hand of my God was on me.

Don't miss the drama in this story! There is an element of audacity in what Nehemiah is requesting of the emperor, and Nehemiah knows it. But the vision God has given him for Jerusalem is too insistent to allow him to remain safely silent. Though he knows he may be risking Artaxerxes's anger or worse, Nehemiah speaks out of the conviction God has planted in his heart, placing his vision before the ruler in the clearest possible terms. And God's grace to Nehemiah is not without effect: Artaxerxes grants his request.

But there is so much more to the story. Good leaders know that the vision must be cast to all those who will be impacted by its realization, even at the risk of discomfort or outright disapproval. And so, we read in the next two verses of Nehemiah chapter 2:

Then I came to the governors of the provinces beyond the Euphrates River and gave them the king's letters. Now the king had sent with me officers of the army and horsemen. And when Sanballat the Horonite and Tobiah the Ammonite official heard about it, it was very displeasing to them that someone had come to seek the welfare of the sons of Israel.

Leaders, and especially those whom God has appointed as overseers, must never forget that the vision, though sent by God, may engender opposition. In fact, it is almost the measure of a vision's importance that there will be those who not only fail to grasp it, but believe it is misplaced or wrong. The truth is that vision never comes without risk attached. But the faithful overseer is able to perceive that the benefits of fulfilling God's mission for the church will always far outweigh the risks and challenges encountered along the way. The overseer must trust that God will remain faithful; God will provide.

Nehemiah's Model for Vision-Casting

Several principles become clear from consideration of Nehemiah's actions thus far, and the first of these is that spiritual leaders cast vision courageously. Remember, Nehemiah had no guarantees that Artaxerxes would receive his request sympathetically. The king could have immediately called for Nehemiah's death, had he chosen to do so. In fact, Nehemiah himself tells us that when he began to make the request, he was "very much afraid." But Nehemiah, prompted by God's spirit and with a prayer on his lips, went ahead and placed his vision for Jerusalem before the king, and he presented it clearly and with all the necessary details to begin its implementation. Not only that, but he was willing to stay true to the vision, even though it would create opposition in some circles.

But casting a vision effectively doesn't stop with the big picture. Reading a little further in Nehemiah chapter 2 shows us that a vision must be clearly articulated, based on "boots on the ground" knowledge of what will be required from those charged with bringing it to fruition.

Spiritual leaders cast vision courageously.

So I came to Jerusalem, and I was there three days. And I got up in the night, I and a few men with me. I did not tell anyone what my God was putting into my mind to do for Jerusalem, and there was no animal with me except the animal on which I was riding. So I went out at night by the Valley Gate in the direction of the Dragon's Spring and on to the Dung Gate, and I was inspecting the walls of Jerusalem which were broken down and its gates which had been consumed by fire. Then I passed on to the Fountain Gate and the King's Pool, but there was no place for my mount to pass. So I was going up at night by the ravine and inspecting the wall. Then I entered the Valley Gate again and returned. However, the officials did not know where I had gone or what I was doing; nor had I as yet told the Jews, the priests, the nobles, the officials, or the rest who were doing the work.

As an overseer charged with a vital mission for God's people, Nehemiah knows that his vision must be complete in every detail. He goes so far as to explore the city by night, when he knows he will be unobserved and undisturbed. He rides all the way around and even dismounts in order to scramble up and down cracked and broken walls and towers because he knows that he must be able to present the vision with the clarity that can only come from detailed observation.

Spiritual leaders craft plans completely.

In other words, the second principle of vision-casting is that spiritual leaders craft plans completely. In addition to the careful pre-planning he did in Susa while in the court of Artaxerxes, Nehemiah took the additional time to closely inspect the walls and buildings in Jerusalem so that he had a complete and accurate grasp of the task that lay before him and could make any modifications necessary. There was nothing half-baked or uninformed about Nehemiah's vision; it was authentic, based firmly on his assessment in real time of the challenges and opportunities involved.

The third principle of effective spiritual leadership is captured in the way Nehemiah goes about communicating the vision to those most directly affected: the people whom he will lead in bringing the vision into reality.

Then I said to them, "You see the bad situation we are in, that Jerusalem is desolate and its gates have been burned by fire. Come, let's build the wall of Jerusalem so that we may no longer be a disgrace." And I told them how the hand of my God had been favorable to me and also about the king's words which he had spoken to me. Then they said, "Let's arise and build." So they put their hands to the good work. But when Sanballat the Horonite and Tobiah the Ammonite official and Geshem the Arab heard about it, they mocked us and despised us and said, "What is this thing that you are doing? Are you rebelling against the king?" So I answered them and said to them, "The God of heaven will make us successful; therefore we his servants will arise and build, but you have no part, right, or memorial in Jerusalem."

Bold words from a faithful heart! Nehemiah is doing what spiritual leaders must do; he is communicating plans carefully. As an overseer, you must always choose your words wisely and well, not only with regard to content, but also considering tone, vernacular, and word choice, because your hearers are affected by each of these elements, whether they realize it or not. Remember, too, that vision language is the most powerful language a leader uses.

Notice that Nehemiah's message to his hearers was precise and specific. In the same way, overseers who are inviting a church to join themselves to the refocusing vision must know:

Spiritual leaders communicate plans carefully.

◊ who they are;

◊ what God is asking;

◊ how they are inviting others to join them in the journey.

Introducing the Refocus Pyramid: The Irreducible Minimums of Leadership Direction

You might remember learning in a geometry or history class that a pyramid is the most structurally stable three-dimensional shape for a given volume. For evidence, you don't need to look any further than the Great Pyramid of Giza in Egypt, which has stood for thousands of years through sandstorms, floods, and even wars.

Similar to the ancient builders of Egypt, an overseer is crafting a structure that is built to last. Though it is a structure built in the minds and hearts of the church, we still desire the greatest stability possible, which makes it logical for us to think of a pyramid as we build and put in place the essential elements of the empowering vision for the church. Our "vision pyramid" has four sides, each of which answers one or more of the six questions each leader must ask and answer in order to succeed in realizing the vision:

 SIDE 1: Mission, Values, and Strategy (the shape of the vision)

◇ What do we do? (mission)

◇ Why do we do it? (values)

◇ How do we do it? (strategy)

 SIDE 2: Vision

◇ Where are we going?

 SIDE 3: Annual Plan

◇ Where do we start?

 SIDE 4: Goals

◇ How do we know if we are making a difference?

> There are
> 6
> irreducible
> minimums
> for leadership.

The answers to these six questions embrace the irreducible minimums of leadership direction. Where church leaders hear these questions clearly and answer with a unified, affirming response, they provide the power of vision to the church. There is excitement, vitality, and energy. This means that as an overseer, you must both answer and empower others to answer these questions clearly, consistently, and with a unified voice if the church is to fulfill the mission God has for it.[1]

"Pastor, I really appreciate the way we're communicating with the church about these new programs; I really do. But I just don't see how we can get enough people involved to handle them. We're already bursting at the seams in Sunday School, my co-teachers and I are tired, and now you're saying that we are going to be asking members to form groups to do all these other things?" Amy Myers shook her head and looked down at the desktop. "I just don't see how we can take all this on right now."

Bob Dunbar clasped his hands together and leaned forward. "Amy, I hear you. And I hear your heart. You've been pouring your heart and soul into our elementary-age kids for years now. You've stepped up when others wouldn't. And I believe God honors your faithfulness.

"But Amy, here's the thing: you, me, and all the rest of us on the leadership team here at Grace have been over the numbers, been over the input from the church members, and been over the comments and ratings from within the team itself. We're doing a great job of bringing along the younger families who've come to Grace Community from other churches—and the children in your classes are proof of that. But there's a huge and growing need in our community for outreach to the people right around our building who've never come through our doors. Our vision for reaching them is clear, and our leadership—including me, as your pastor—is convinced that this is an open door God is placing before us. Amy, do you believe that God still provides for his people?"

"Of course I do."

"That's what I knew you'd say. I believe it, too. And I believe that God is going to raise up the people we need to make his vision for our church a reality." Bob grinned. "He might even bring along an assistant Sunday School department head. You certainly deserve the help."

The Mission—What Do We Do?

At this point, some reading this may be thinking something along these lines: "All this talk about vision, mission, strategy, goals, and all the rest sounds like it comes more from some business leadership self-help book than from the Bible. Are we following Jesus, or are we just 'spiritualizing' some secular principles?"

It is certainly true that some churches have done something like this. But I want to encourage you to see and understand that God has always been in the business of vision-casting for his people. In fact, we find in scripture abundant examples of how God has provided a vision, how he has formed mission in the minds of the church, how he has planted values in faithful hearts, and how strategy, goals, and planning have been developed to support the mission and bring the vision into reality.

Jesus Announces the Mission

In Matthew 28:18–20, we read these words:

> And Jesus came up and spoke to them, saying, "All authority in heaven and on earth has been given to me. Go therefore and make disciples of all the nations, baptizing them in the name of the Father and the Son and the Holy Spirit, teaching them to follow all that I have commanded you. And behold, I am with you always, to the end of the age."

Could Christ have been any clearer about the mission he has given the church? "Go," "make disciples," "baptize," "teach"… each of these is a missional directive from the Lord, and they come with the guarantee that the risen Christ himself will go with us, empowering us to carry out the work that he has called the church to do. In fact, each of the gospel accounts of Jesus' ministry on the earth contains, at or near its end, some version of this statement from Jesus, announcing his mission for the church.

God Defines the Church's Values

If you want to understand the values that drove the vision of the church in its earliest days, all you need to do is look at Acts 2:42–47:

> They were continually devoting themselves to the apostles' teaching and to fellowship, to the breaking of bread and to prayers. Everyone kept feeling a sense of awe; and many wonders and signs were taking place through the apostles. And all the believers were together and had all things in common; and they would sell their property and possessions and share them with all, to the extent that anyone had need. Day by day, continuing with one mind in the Temple and breaking bread from house to house, they were taking their meals together with gladness and sincerity of heart, praising God and having favor with all the people. And the Lord was adding to their number day by day those who were being saved.

In the Book of Acts, there are seven summary statements where the values of the church are clearly articulated. The first of these is found in the passage above, Acts 2:42–47. This is also the longest and most well-known expression of the church's values in the Book of Acts. Reading these words, it's not difficult to pick up on what the earliest Christians valued most: teaching, fellowship, breaking bread together, prayer, signs and wonders, and taking care of each other by sharing possessions. No wonder they enjoyed such a good opinion from "all the people." And there are six similar statements in the Book of Acts, where the values of the church are described.

As we can see from this biblical example, identifying what the church values as well as what distinguishes your church from other churches is an essential part of providing leadership to the church body.

Jesus Lays Out His Strategy

The Lord had a clear strategy for how he would make and form disciples, outlined in the four statements he made as he called them unto himself: "Come and see," "follow me," "abide in me," and finally, "go and tell." In fact, the early church reflected this same pattern of inviting in / sending out by following the blueprint outlined by Jesus as described by his words in Acts 1:8:

> ... *You will receive power when the Holy Spirit has come upon you; and you shall be my witnesses both in Jerusalem, and in all Judea and Samaria, and as far as the remotest part of the earth."*

In such passages, we can discern both the personal strategy of Jesus for making followers and the geographic strategy that guided the church in taking His message to the entire known world.

God's Vision for His People

Without question, scripture is full of announcements of God's vision for his people. One of the most dramatic examples is found in Revelation 7:9–12:

> *After these things, I looked, and behold, a great multitude which no one could count, from every nation and all tribes and peoples and languages, standing before the throne and before the Lamb ... and they cried out with a loud voice, saying, "Salvation belongs to our God who sits on the throne, and to the Lamb" ... and they fell on their faces before the throne and worshiped God, saying, "Amen, blessing and glory and wisdom and thanksgiving and honor and power and might, be to our God forever and ever. Amen."*

I remember when it first hit me that this scripture captures God's vision for all of us. I was working with a church leadership team, and we were trying to gain an understanding of what vision truly is and how it functions to propel a church's forward progress. I realized that in this vision from the Apostle John, we see a vivid portrait of what God's vision is for his people. What a thing to contemplate! Here, at the end of all things, is what God most wants to see: all His people, from every corner of the world He created, gathered in worship and adoration. This ultimate vision is what animates and empowers God's church to pursue its mission—announced by Jesus himself—of making disciples throughout the world.

CHAPTER 4

Mission Informs the Mind

It is vital for overseers to be clear about the function of the mission: it answers the question, "What do we do?" It informs the mind, helping us understand who we are, whom we serve, what problems we're trying to solve, and what the end goal or transformational destination looks like. The mission is here and now; it provides the day-to-day direction that keeps us focused on the objective.[2]

Often, in my work with churches, I have found that pastors and other church leaders have difficulty differentiating between mission and vision. I have been asked if they are really two different things, or if both are really needed. My answer is that both are absolutely vital for refocusing and revitalizing the church. They are two different things and accomplish two different outcomes, and the distinctions must be clear and well communicated. *Mission* captures what we intend to do; it is a hard-working, "blue-collar" reminder of our duty. *Vision* inspires us to go where God is leading; it is an aspirational statement that inspires the heart. The overseer's vision for the church typically should include three components: a vision *tagline*, a vision *statement*, and a vision *description*.

For this reason, it is vital for overseers leading churches through the refocusing process to help them develop the *mission statement:* a modern restatement of the Great Commission, customized and tailored to fit your church. As the overseer charged with guiding and protecting the flock under your care, and as a steward of Christ's mission, you have few more crucial tasks than distilling your church's mission into a short, meaningful, and specific statement that captures your church's "big idea"—your church's, specifically, not a statement borrowed from another church. Your mission statement should also reflect the principal qualities of the mission:

> A church's *mission statement* is a modern restatement of the Great Commission, customized to fit your church.

◇ Express strategic intent;

◇ Resonate in the hearts of those you lead;

64

◇   Provide focus for ministry;

◇   Inform decision-making;

◇   Offer a rallying point for the church;

◇   Inform strategy;

◇   Provide a standard for measurement and evaluation of ministry effectiveness.

Values—Why Do We Do It?

As we saw from the example in Acts 2:42–47, the earliest Christians had a clear set of values that informed their mission. The value they placed on the apostles' teaching, close fellowship and mutual caring, and the other qualities and activities mentioned dictated the character of their mission to Jerusalem, Judea, Samaria, and "the remotest part of the earth."

The fact is that every church has a set of values, whether stated or not. They govern the way a church lives, how it conducts its activities, and even the types of conversations members have with each other and with church leaders. It is an essential part of the discovery process for overseers to have a clear understanding, not only of their own values as pastors but also of the shared, communal values of the church. I cannot emphasize this strongly enough: *no mission can extend beyond the boundaries of a church's values.* Alignment of mission and values is essential.

It's also important for overseers to understand that there is a difference between a church's *articulated* values and its *aspirational* values. The former are those values that have already been absorbed, propagated, and acted upon; the latter are values that the church desires to have or believes must be valued even when they are not currently present. As part of the revitalization process, an aspirational value may be considered, but it must be clearly identified as such, both by the overseer and the church.

The most important values consideration for overseers and churches seeking revitalization is that there must be a forward-oriented expression of core values in order for the church to move forward on the mission. This is because what the church currently values is producing the results that have led to the need for church revitalization. This, in fact, is the greatest challenge of values

65

expression in church revitalization. The correct core values must be identified, but they must be positioned with a forward and future orientation.

A church's core values possess several characteristics:

◇ They change slowly;

◇ They are things the church is passionate about;

◇ They are rooted in the Bible;

◇ They are foundational beliefs;

◇ They guide the church.

On the other hand, core values are not simply a list of everything the church believes. Rather, they are four to seven essential or foundational elements that the church is built upon. For churches seeking revitalization, identifying and developing core values is essential. One of the most common reasons churches fall into decline is because their values are not in alignment with the mission God has provided (for examples of churches needing realigned values, re-read Revelation chapters 2 and 3). Another problem arises when the values of the overseer and the church are out of alignment. After all, personal values don't always match organizational values. In fact, different parts of the same church can have different values (what we refer to as "departmental values"). Misaligned values create stress in the church and in the pastor. Revitalized churches have core values that align across the broad spectrum, from the youngest members to the oldest, and from the pastor down to the people in the pews. In declining churches, core values are more important to identify and lead out of. This is because decision-making in a growth posture is about what we do next, but leading on the back side of the growth curve requires core values to be clear, so they are not violated unnecessarily.

The correct core values must be identified, but they must be positioned with a forward and future orientation.

For this reason, overseers must perform careful, methodical assessment to understand and gain agreement on the core values—especially those unstated or unconscious values that, despite often having never been overtly expressed, still exercise great sway over the behavior and direction of the church. For the church's unity and thriving in its mission, alignment on core values is a must.

Strategy—How Do We Do It?

Leading on the back side of the growth curve requires core values to be clear so they are not violated unnecessarily.

One of my favorite memories as a kid was going to Shoney's Restaurant with my family, because they had placemats with activities for kids to do during the seemingly interminable wait for the food to arrive. I loved the dot-to-dot puzzles; my sister and I would race to see who could finish the fastest (I guess I've always been a little bit competitive). And I still remember the satisfaction of finding the next dot and seeing the pattern emerge.

Strategy is where the church begins to "connect the dots" and begins pursuing and completing the mission. It answers the "how do we do it?" question by laying out the steps for each church's individual fulfillment of the Great Commission. Strategy, when conceived properly, is both a process and a roadmap; it gives us clarity on what needs to happen and when, and it also helps us see the route to the final destination.

As framed by Jesus, the mission destination is focused on making disciples "of all nations"; likewise, that must be the ultimate aim for each revitalized church in every community. This means, however, that two essential questions must be answered in order to develop an effective strategy for your church:

1. What is a disciple?

2. How will we design our ministry to make disciples?

CHAPTER 4

One definition of "disciple" might be something like this: *A disciple is a person who lives life daily in ways compatible with the life and teachings of Christ.* In fact, this is how John defines discipleship in his first epistle:

> *By this we may know that we are in him: the one who says*
> *that he remains in him ought, himself also, to walk just as He*
> *walked (1 John 2:5,6).*

Think about what is required to "walk as Jesus did": a person must have knowledge and understanding of biblical teaching as well as familiarity with the life, teaching, actions, and commands of Christ. In other words, discipleship involves a lifestyle and habits that are informed by and flow out of a daily, personal relationship with Jesus Christ.

Next, think about how Jesus himself went about forming disciples. We've already mentioned his four-part strategy: 1) come and see; 2) follow me; 3) abide in me; 4) go and tell. The beautiful aspect of this strategy is that when executed well, it becomes self-propagating. The apostles came and saw; they followed; they learned how to abide in the life and spirit of Christ; and all these experiences impelled them to go and tell others, beginning the process over again as they invited others to "come and see."

But each church must design its own unique strategy for making disciples, and it is the task of an overseer to guide the church toward an individualized disciple-making ministry that takes full consideration of the church's "big idea," the needs of the surrounding community, and the passion and direction of leadership, all guided by the empowering vision. The way your church attracts, develops, and sends out disciples cannot be modeled on how another church does it; your strategy must be tailored to your specific situation.

Now, this does not mean that there aren't some general principles that should be understood and employed when developing your church's strategy for moving people from a state of unbelief (unconverted) to new birth (conversion), followed by development (growth) and maturity in Christ (deployed for making new disciples). In fact, there are five elements that should be considered when developing the strategy:

1. How will you reach your community?

2. How will you plan to make disciples?

3. How will you develop leaders?

4. What will you ask your people to do?

5. What does a mature follower of Jesus look like?

In my experience working with churches, I've found that developing a strategy that really works sustainably takes some time. Adjustments will be necessary; changes will have to be made in some areas. Overseers should be prepared to tweak, to assess which elements require attention. Sometimes you may need to change or replace elements one at a time to get the whole in proper alignment. Getting to a refined, dependable strategy can take a year or two.[3]

Some overseers may find it helpful to think of a design for their strategy that breaks it into three phases with keywords, such as "engage, embrace, equip," or "commission, connect, commit." Conceiving the disciple-making strategy in this way may also better enable you to develop creative solutions and processes for each phase, leading to a better understanding by the church and better acceptance and implementation. Refer to the *Strategy* design examples (*Image 6*) on the following page.

It's also helpful to remember that though your "big" strategy, once it is fully implemented, will not change, you may also need to employ mini-strategies within certain ministries or departments of your church. But these must always be supportive of, derived from, and informed by the "big strategy" that is driving the church toward fulfillment of God's mission.

We've covered a lot of territory in this chapter, but remember, casting the vision for an effective mission—one based on the church's core values and employing the right strategy for your unique circumstances—is fundamental to everything else that will follow in the revitalization process. Overseers should take heart: by building your church's mission around the Great Commission announced by Jesus, and by harnessing the power of values to a strategy that proceeds from Jesus' own plan for disciple-making, you are following the path God has laid out for the accomplishment of His great vision for all creation.

(Image 6)

THE PYRAMID | Mission - Values - STRATEGY

EXAMPLES

EXAMPLE 1

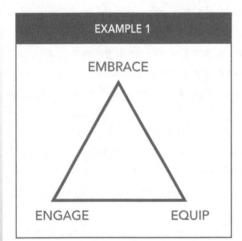

EXAMPLE 2

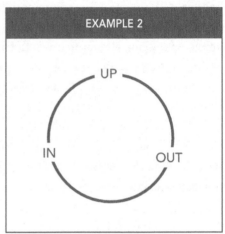

EXAMPLE 3

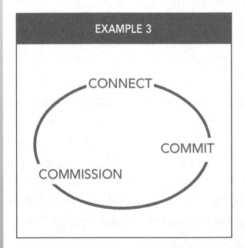

EXAMPLE 4

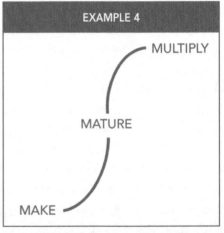

Notes

1. I am deeply indebted to Will Mancini for his teaching about the "vision frame" and how it shapes vision, as presented in his book *Church Unique: How Missional Leaders Cast Vision, Capture Culture, and Create Movement* (Jossey-Bass, 2008). Likewise, Aubrey Malphurs, in *Values-Driven Leadership: Discovering and Developing Your Core Values for Ministry* (Baker, 2004), describes how vision must always remain within the boundaries dictated by values. Finally, Patrick Lencioni's "Establishing a Thematic Goal Road Map" describes how to develop a theme with supporting component parts. Each of these resources helped form the foundation and concepts for the *ReFocus* four-sided pyramid.

2. Michael Hyatt's *The Vision-Driven Leader* (Baker, 2020) is an excellent resource for pastors and churches for differentiating between vision and mission and how the two function together.

3. The process of experimentation and refinement resembles the Flywheel Concept first introduced by Jim Collins in his book, *Good to Great*; the strategy development process involves a lot of effort in the initial stages and builds on various levels of input and development, much like setting a giant flywheel in motion. But once the "breakthrough" moment is achieved, momentum builds and the process becomes more self-sustaining. Jesus' four-part strategy, predating Jim Collins by 2,000 years, exhibits many of the same characteristics. He spent intensive time with those he called, but when the "breakthrough moment" came on the Day of Pentecost, the disciple-making process spread with irresistible force.

CHAPTER

5

Explode Your Vision

Getting vision right, both for the overseer and for those being led, is more difficult than you might imagine. If you need proof, look no farther than the story of Joseph in the Old Testament. Early in Joseph's life, God revealed to Joseph that he was a visionary. Joseph saw two visions that God used to teach him about vision casting: lessons that Joseph needed to learn! Without question, Joseph's early vision-casting was powerful, but it was also provocative because he did not yet understand the power and possibilities of vision.

You will recall that Joseph's first vision was of eleven sheaves bowing down to his sheaf (Genesis 37:5–8). Though the vision would eventually become reality, Joseph's brothers hated him for his vision. They said, "Are you actually going to reign over us?" I am sure this caused no small disturbance within Joseph's home, and Joseph's mother likely took notice, even to the point of running interference for Joseph.

But things got worse when Joseph had another dream. Failing to learn the lesson about how to cast vision, Joseph recounted his second dream, in which the sun, moon, and eleven stars bowed down to Joseph's star (Genesis 37:9–11). The Bible recounts how even Joseph's parents were dismayed by this instance of Joseph's vision-casting. You might say that Joseph struggled to understand the power of vision and also with the issues of self-focused vision casting.

In other words, Joseph failed to understand what so many leaders fail to understand: the power and process of vision-casting and of accomplishing the vision that has been cast. Joseph did not lose his ability to cast vision over the next few decades of his life, but what he did lose was his selfish focus. It required his enslavement, imprisonment, and a period of time during which he may have wondered whether he had been forgotten in order for Joseph to learn that vision is not about the leader. Rather, vision is about how God can use a spiritual leader to accomplish His plans and fulfill His mission.

An overseer's most basic task is casting a vision that is clear, that captures the future, aspirational destination for the church, and that serves to bring together the passions of members and the open door God is placing before the church. Vision-casting animates the church's mission, gives it direction, is formed by its values, and orders its strategic priorities.

Where Are We Going?

Above all, vision answers the basic question, "Where are we going?" When you think about it, what could be more foundational for any kind of leader than making sure those being led are clear on where they're going? As an overseer, you must always avoid the syndrome expressed by engineer and author Linda Robinson: "I must catch up to the others, for I am their leader."

Fortunately for us, the Bible provides plentiful examples of both poor and God-anointed leadership. As we explore more fully the nature, importance, and components of developing and sharing your vision for the church, it's helpful to remind ourselves of the people we want to emulate.

Joseph: His Vision for a Crucial Time of Need

As we've already seen, Joseph clearly had some early problems with knowing how, when, and in what words to do his vision-casting. On the other hand, once we remember "the rest of the story," we can't deny that Joseph was both an overseer and an overcomer! Led by his trust in God, Joseph was ultimately able to utilize his powers of envisioning God's future for his people to go from the dungeons of Egypt to the right hand of the Pharaoh himself. And along the way, he saved thousands of lives—including those of his family.

In Genesis chapter 41 we read the story of Pharaoh's troubling dream. His cupbearer, formerly Joseph's cellmate, upon hearing about his ruler's discomfort, remembered the Hebrew youth who had successfully interpreted his dream in prison, two years earlier. He recommended that Pharaoh send for Joseph:

> *Pharaoh said to Joseph: "I have had a dream, and there is no one who can interpret it; and I have heard it said about you that when you hear a dream you can interpret it." Joseph then answered*

Pharaoh, saying, "It has nothing to do with me; God will give Pharaoh an answer for his own good."

After listening to Pharaoh's dream, Joseph told him what was about to take place and about how the upcoming seven years of plentiful harvests would be followed by seven years of disastrous famine, assuring him,

> *"... the matter is confirmed by God, and God will quickly bring it about. So now let Pharaoh look for a man discerning and wise, and appoint him over the land of Egypt. Let Pharaoh take action to appoint overseers in charge of the land and let him take a fifth of the produce of the land of Egypt as a tax in the seven years of abundance. Then have them collect all the food of these good years that are coming and store up grain for food in the cities... Let the food be used as a reserve for the land for the seven years of famine which will occur in the land of Egypt, so that the land will not perish through the famine." Now the proposal seemed good to Pharaoh and to all his servants. Then Pharaoh said to his servants, "Can we find a man like this, in whom there is a divine spirit?"*

Quick to recognize Joseph's qualities, Pharaoh placed him over the vast effort of organizing the gathering and storage of food for the entire nation. In fact, Pharaoh made Joseph the second-most powerful leader in Egypt.

In the story of Joseph's ascent to power, we see the essential elements of how an overseer casts a vision. By the power of God's spirit, Joseph not only saw what was coming; he also saw what needed to happen. His vision was clear; it included a carefully detailed mission and strategy; and Joseph provided an unambiguous description of what a successful outcome would look like.

Proverbs 29:18 says, "Where there is no vision, the people perish" (KJV). In this case, vast numbers of people would have no doubt perished in the absence of the empowering, animating vision provided by God through Joseph. In the same way, churches in decline risk the fate of irrelevance or worse when there is no overseer who can provide God's vision for the church's revitalization.

God's Grand Vision

We have already seen the beautiful, worship-inspiring portrayal of God's ultimate vision for all His people as described by the apostle John in Revelation 7:9–11. When God's vision is realized, people from "all tribes and peoples and languages" will stand before His throne in full-throated worship. God's vision is the culmination of the mission the risen Christ proclaimed to His disciples when He said, in Matthew 28:19, "Go therefore and make disciples of all nations," baptizing them and teaching them to live according to the Lord's instruction.

As an overseer, your task is to call your church to fulfill its part in bringing about the realization of God's vision for all humankind. Like Joseph, you must listen closely to the promptings of the Holy Spirit and be prepared to announce the vision in terms that your church will understand, implant in their hearts and imaginations, and dedicate themselves to carrying out.

This last point bears further examination. I cannot stress enough how vital it is to do everything possible to engage the hearts and imaginations of your church. The fact is that it is difficult for all of us to raise our eyes above the level of the day-to-day in order to catch a glimpse of the promises held by the envisioned future. The vision must be aspirational, but most of us live our lives in the here and now, overcoming problems and taking care of the tasks required to keep our lives on track—paying bills, going to work, raising children, and investing in our relationships with our spouses.

But when you're concerned with paying bills today, it can be hard to contemplate longer-term goals like retirement or a long-anticipated, special vacation. That's why it's important to have a vision for the ultimate destination or goal to which we aspire—to keep our hearts encouraged for the daily struggle; to periodically lift our eyes above the plain of "what is" and catch a glimpse of the mountain peaks of "what will be." As an overseer, you will need to help your church stay motivated and committed to the goal through some potentially difficult and confusing passages. A dynamic vision that grips the heart and excites the imagination is the most valuable resource you can have for maintaining forward momentum in the revitalization process.

Pastor Jim Thomas listened carefully as Robert McCormick continued speaking. Robert, a longtime member of Sanford

Memorial, had asked for a time to meet with Jim about "some things I've been thinking about for a few weeks."

When Robert had made his request, Jim didn't miss the significance of the time frame for Robert's period of contemplation. It had been about five weeks since Jim, backed by his advisory team, had announced their vision for the church's next five years. It was a bold vision that required the reallocation of some existing resources and a commitment to finding new ones, and Jim Thomas knew that among certain circles in the church, concerns were being expressed. People were worried, among other things, about paying for "Pastor Jim's plans," and though Jim knew that the vast majority of the advisory team was on board, not everyone in the church felt the same way.

"I've been a member here at Sanford for a long time," Robert McCormick was saying, "and I've seen a lot of people come and go. I've seen a few pastors come and go, too," he said, meeting Jim's gaze squarely. "I'm all for seeing the church move forward, but..." Robert's voice fell silent, but his implication was clear.

Jim allowed himself several seconds before replying. "Robert, I appreciate you coming here and laying all this out for me. And I can hear the concern in your words. You're worried about how a church of our relatively small size is going to be able to do everything we've been talking about. And I can see why you'd feel that way; it's a lot to think about."

"Yes, it is," McCormick said quickly, "and I keep thinking about what Jesus said when he talked about someone who starts building a tower and then can't finish it. I just don't want to see something like that happen to this church."

Pastor Thomas nodded thoughtfully. "Robert, I hear you, I sure do. And yet, I wonder which direction you're looking."

Robert gave him a confused look.

"I've heard folks like you and Esther Callan talk about some of the problems the church has had, even before I came here. There have been a few things the church tried that didn't work out, isn't that right?"

McCormick nodded.

"But Robert, we can't let the obstacles and problems of the past dictate the future for our church," Jim said. "When Jesus talked about not starting something that you can't finish, he wasn't talking about the church and its mission. Remember, he also said that the gates of Hell itself wouldn't overcome the church, and he promised to be with us all the way to the end of the age."

Robert McCormick wore a thoughtful expression.

"Robert, I've described for the church the process that we've been going through as we've developed these plans. And every step of the way, we've bathed this process in prayer, seeking the Lord's will—not asking him to anoint our plans, but rather to reveal his plan for this church to us, so that we could get about the business of fulfilling the Great Commission. This vision that we share is not something I dreamed up, Robert. It's not the blueprint for a tower that I want to build. No, sir, I believe with all my heart that this is something God wants to do through our church.

"And Robert, as your pastor, I'm asking for your trust. I know that a lot of folks are looking ahead and can't see how we can do all this. But remember: faith means that sometimes, you keep walking even when you aren't sure where the path is leading. I believe that as we continue to walk in faith, God is going to make everything plain. But to get where we're going, we've got to keep taking steps."

In every church seeking revitalization, overseers are going to know people like Robert McCormick. Perhaps the most effective way to deal sensitively with those sincere individuals who confess misgivings about the church's direction is to have a firm grasp of the vision. This is your church's "preview of coming attractions"—or maybe it would be more accurate to say "preview of coming victory."

Vision Inspires the Heart

The quality of vision that provides its power is its ability to inspire and even change the heart. People with inspired hearts are capable of accomplishing amazing things.

In 1730, a church in Sussex, England, posted a sign with these words: "A vision without a task is but a dream; a task without a vision is drudgery; but a vision and a task are the hope of the world." So true! The day-to-day tasks that comprise the mission must be harnessed to and driven by the energizing, inspiring vision that captures the ultimate goal.

Vision that is capable of empowering lasting change possesses several key characteristics:

1. **Vision creates excitement.** When the church is genuinely enthusiastic about reaching the goal captured in the vision, that energy can alleviate feelings of drudgery, worry, and doubt that often stand in the way of accomplishment.

2. **Vision gives purpose.** People who share a common vision are able to get past personal differences in opinion and personality in order to get things done.

3. **Vision provides inspiration.** Please don't underestimate the importance of inspiration and the way it can keep the church and its leaders motivated and focused.

4. **Vision empowers leaders.** One of the chief qualities an overseer must possess is the ability to both receive a vision and to bequeath it to others. That "looking-forward" quality is what distinguishes mediocre leaders from great ones.

5. ***Vision promotes excellence.*** When a church knows where it is going, its people are more willing to "cast aside everything that hinders," in the words of Paul, in order to pursue the cherished goal.

6. ***Vision encourages giving.*** People who are passionate about a vision are willing to give time, treasure, and talent in service of the goal. Having discovered "the pearl of great price," they will "sell out" in order to obtain it.

7. ***Vision creates a journey.*** Perhaps one of the most important things about a vision is the way it orients us toward what is to come, rather than looking back at past failures or problems. When we are looking ahead to the fulfillment of the vision, we are more likely to stay on the path that leads us there.

As you guide your church toward its empowering vision, you must first come to clarity, both with yourself and with your key team members, about the nature of the vision. Remember, to be effective, a vision must both be clear in the minds of the church and must proceed out of and be informed by the church's core values. To that end, and depending on the needs and values of your church, a vision may be of several types.

◇ **GOSPEL SATURATION**—In Acts 13, we read an account of the vision exercised by the leaders of the church in Antioch. Under the guidance of the Holy Spirit, they had a vision for seeing the gospel proclaimed as widely as possible.

◇ **TRANSFORMATIONAL TEACHING**—Acts 18:25–27 portrays the teaching vision of the faithful Ephesian couple Priscilla and Aquilla. Their sensitive and thorough instruction of the gifted evangelist Apollos resulted in the transformation of a powerful ministry.

◇ **LEADERSHIP FORMATION**—The letters from
Paul to Titus and Timothy illustrate Paul's vision for the
establishment of faithful leaders in all the churches. He
urged his younger protégés to appoint and train overseers
capable of guarding and leading the faithful in their
communities.

◇ **INSTITUTIONAL CHANGE OR
TRANSFORMATION**—In John 4, we read the tender
story of Jesus and the Samaritan woman at the well. It is
significant that here, for the first time, Jesus announces
both His Messiahship and His intention to transform the
institutions and understanding of faithful worship when
He says, "... the hour is coming when ... true worshipers
will worship the Father in spirit and truth..." In fact, a
vision for institutional change in a church will often result
in yet another vision, based on the nature of the change
being sought.

◇ **MEETING A CRISIS**—Acts 6 provides insight into
perhaps the first crisis within the early church, when the
Greek-speaking widows were being neglected in the daily
food distribution. In fact, there are two visions in play
here: the apostles' need, as stated in Acts 6:2, to remain
focused on their vision for teaching and prayer; and the
vision for unity among the believers as a powerful witness
to the surrounding community. In both cases, the nature
of the vision dictated the steps taken to achieve it.

◇ **ENJOYING GOD'S PRESENCE**—The prophet
Jeremiah announced a vision for all humanity to draw
near to God when he said, in 31:34, that in days to come,
"No longer shall one teach his neighbor... saying, 'Know

the Lord,' for they shall all know me, from the least of them to the greatest, declares the Lord."

◇ **REPRODUCTION AND MULTIPLICATION**—In his letter to the Christians in Thessalonica, Paul praises their vision for replicating their faith throughout the region, calling them "an example to all the believers in Macedonia and Achaia... Your faith in God has gone forth everywhere..." (1 Thessalonians 1:7,8).

◇ **MINISTRY MOBILIZATION**—When Jesus sent His followers out to preach, He provided not only the vision for their work but also the mission and strategies they should follow. In Luke 9:1–2, we read that He gave them power and commissioned them to "proclaim the kingdom of God." Upon receiving their mobilizing vision, they departed and "began going throughout the villages, preaching the Gospel and healing everywhere."

And these are not by any means all the forms that a vision can take. The point is, understanding what type of vision your church will pursue is an essential starting point.

This is where your work in understanding *The Convergence* begins to pay off. By knowing your church's "big idea" and seeing the "sweet spot" where leadership passion, community need, and the purpose of the church overlap, your vision will be integrated with and responsive to the church's local fulfillment of the Great Commission.

Vision Statement

Though we often hear businesses and other organizations talk about their vision statements, here, too, the church is following the well-established practice outlined in scripture. As you develop the vision statement for your church, it will be important to go back and look again at what you learned during your processes of *Discovery* and *Convergence*. Consider what elements of your *Convergence* need to be linked to your vision statement.

Ideally, the vision statement for your church should be eight words (or less) that capture a compelling picture of the future of your church as it carries out Jesus's mission in the world. It should encompass the key elements of your *Convergence* "sweet spot" and should be grounded in the church's core values.

- ◇ "Bringing the joy of Jesus to our city"

- ◇ "Helping people live for more"

- ◇ "Partnering with people so they find the way home"

- ◇ "Speaking the peace of God into the brokenness of the world"

- ◇ "Offering the rest of Jesus Christ to a restless community"

Some key questions to ask yourself and your vision and advisory teams as you develop your vision statement include:

- ◇ Can this be our church's rallying cry?

- ◇ Will the majority of our members identify with this vision?

- ◇ Is this statement "big enough"?

- ◇ Can this statement serve and empower the church for the next five to seven years?

- ◇ Does our senior leadership rally around this statement?

If "yes" isn't the answer to all of these questions, you need to keep working until your leadership team is in complete agreement.

Vision Objectives

Once your vision statement has taken shape, the next crucial step is to develop a plan to bring the vision to fulfillment. A little later on, in addition to your vision objectives, we'll discuss developing an annual plan and its supporting elements to provide specific direction and concrete steps toward bringing the vision to reality. But for now, we want to focus on the objectives you'll need in order to keep progress toward the vision goals on track.

The goal of articulating the vision objectives is to build momentum. After all, one of the greatest challenges in church revitalization is overcoming negative momentum. Developing big, momentum-changing objectives is essential to arresting a church's decline. The compounding effects of positive momentum for three to five years are required to overcome the negative effect of decline.

Remember that the vision statement captures where you intend for the ministry to be in five to seven years. Your vision objectives, on the other hand, provide the focus and direction for the intermediate steps toward fulfillment: one year at a time. These objectives will form the structure for your church's annual plan, and each annual plan will also contain components we'll refer to as "elements": the elements will be 30, 60, and/or 90 days of focus that lead to the fulfillment of the annual plan (or objective). Note that the objective under the vision is the same as the annual plan at the top of the pyramid.

Refer to the *Vision Pyramid (Image 7)* on the following page.

Establishing and accomplishing the elements will help you assess your progress and ensure that the church is moving steadily toward the fulfillment of the vision.

To develop objectives, it's often helpful for overseers to brainstorm with the vision team. At this stage, don't focus too much on the sequence or try to make final decisions about where in the five- to seven-year vision cycle each objective falls. Just get down the main objectives that will be required to see the vision realized, remembering that your objectives are the big, church-wide efforts that will organize and direct your efforts for each year. You should aim to develop six to ten potential objectives that can then be further refined.[1]

Vision Tagline

For most churches, a vision tagline is also important. This should be a more compact version of the vision statement that captures its essence. In fact, I know of one church that was able to boil its five-word vision statement down to a single word: "Ask."

As with everything else related to your vision statement, it should be crafted in view of everything you've learned so far and take into account the feedback you've gotten from your vision and advisory teams.

(Image 7)

THE PYRAMID | Vision

On the diagram below, write the vision statement and objectives you built through the previous exercises.

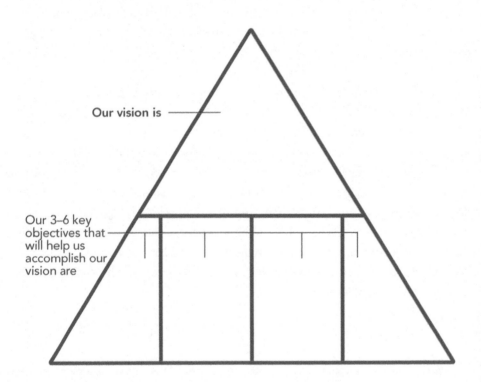

Our vision is ————

Our 3–6 key objectives that will help us accomplish our vision are

Vision Paragraphs

For larger churches or those with more complex needs, I recommend also creating vision paragraphs. These should be two to four paragraphs that more fully describe the complete vision for the church. They should expand on the vision statement with additional details, including what fulfillment of the vision looks and feels like and how the vision fulfillment is celebrated. Overseers, as you craft these paragraphs, take great care to carefully consider all the feedback you've received from your leadership teams and what you've learned in your *Discovery* and *Convergence* processes.

Ultimately, the vision paragraph should be cast in language that is authentic to you and reflective of the way you teach, pray, and counsel with your church. It should inspire your church to "reach forward" toward the fulfillment of the vision and provide aspirational imagery to propel and inspire the church's efforts.

The Power of Expressing a Vision

At this point, some may be wondering, "Is it really worth all this trouble, coming up with a vision statement, then a tagline and paragraphs? Is it overkill? Can't we just announce the vision and let it go at that?"

It's true that vision-casting is hard work, and discussions about getting the terminology "just right" can easily deteriorate into unprofitable word parsing and overthinking. But I want to stress once again that nothing in the entire revitalization process is more powerful than the empowering vision. Remember the words of the church in Sussex: the vision gives life and energy to the task, and the task brings the vision to fulfillment. You can't have one without the other.

Remember also the time-tested proverb: "Repetition is the mother of learning." After all the prayerful work the overseer has put in, both individually and with the leadership teams, the vision may seem like second nature. But the people in the pews of your church—those who must actually put their hands to the plow and not look back—will need to re-experience the vision multiple times before it becomes ingrained and accepted as part of the "corporate DNA."

Encourage Stewardship

Keep in mind that the vision, when expressed well and consistently, encourages more thoughtful use of the time, talent, and treasure each of your church members has been entrusted with by God. It is a well-known principle that people are more motivated to give by a vision than they are by "meeting a need." By carefully crafting your vision and consistently placing it before the church, you are helping your fellow believers remain passionately engaged in resourcing the church.

Inspire Hearts

While the mission and its various objectives inform the mind ("How do we do it?"), the vision inspires the heart ("Where are we going?"). Nothing is more inspiring than the sense of journeying together toward a cherished destination or experiencing the achievement of our desires. Overseers can think of the vision as the "north star" that keeps the church looking forward in anticipation as they face the daily tasks of the mission.

Energize Leadership

What could be more discouraging to a leader than not knowing where they are taking their followers? Exemplified by the question, "What am I doing?" on Pastor Bob's whiteboard, a lack of leadership confidence is fatal to any organization if allowed to go unaddressed. By contrast, a clear vision that has been communicated with skill and consistency is, for leadership, the "gift that keeps on giving." It inspires confidence and sets priorities.

Lead Change

Supposedly, someone once asked the great artist Michaelangelo how he went about creating his masterpiece, the monumental statue of David that stands in the Academy in Florence, Italy. Michaelangelo is said to have replied, "I saw the figure of David residing in the block of marble, and I simply took away everything that didn't look like the figure." In the same way, a clear vision provides an effective matrix for leadership decisions about necessary changes. Churches going through the revitalization process will inevitably encounter situations where long-standing, even cherished practices of the church must be changed in order to make way for the fulfillment of the vision. We all know that change is hard, but when it is guided by a steady vision for what is to come, the need for change is easier to communicate and more likely to be accepted by the church.

I hope that by now you are well on your way toward developing the empowering vision for your church. Never forget that in doing so, you stand in the lineage of great biblical leaders like Joseph, Nehemiah, and Jesus Christ Himself.

Think for a moment about what it means to be an "overseer." Your task is to look above and beyond, not only keeping an eye on the flock within your care, but also searching the horizon for what lies ahead. By developing, announcing, and facilitating the full acceptance of the vision for your church, you are guiding them toward the place where they can fully participate in the saving work of Christ in the world. You are helping them to become, both individually and corporately, all that Jesus intends for them to be. There can be no greater work.

Notes

1. This exercise is adapted from Patrick Lencioni's *Silos, Politics, and Turf Wars: A Leadership Fable about Destroying the Barriers That Turn Colleagues into Competitors* (Jossey-Bass, 2006).

CHAPTER
6

An Annual Ministry Plan
Gets You Going

The praise team ended the final chorus. Pastor Ken smiled broadly and signaled for the church to be seated as he approached the lectern. He arranged his sermon outline, opened his Bible to the first passage, and set it to one side.

He invited the church to prayer and recited his customary pre-sermon benediction: "Father God, may the words of my mouth and the meditations of our hearts be pleasing in your sight. May your message speak through me, and may all our hearts be empowered with understanding by your Holy Spirit. Amen."

He took one more look at his outline. His purpose today was to place before Gilead Bible Church the process that was necessary to get on the path to revitalization—to taking up the mission that God was placing before them. The path was clear in Ken's mind; it made sense, each step was the logical outgrowth of the previous one. But could he present it today in a way that allowed these people to see it with the same clarity, the same inevitability?

He had chosen for his text the story of Jonah, the prophet who had tried to avoid God's call to a difficult mission by running away. Ken knew that for the process to unfold for this church, they must first hear and accept God's call, even if that challenged what they thought they knew about the mission of the church in the world. Until they heard and received this first truth, nothing else would matter.

Lord, open my mouth, Ken prayed silently, *and open our hearts.* He began reading aloud from Jonah, chapter one.

Getting Off the Ground

As you begin to turn from accepting and clarifying the vision and move toward preparing to implement the on-the-ground objectives that will carry your church forward, you will begin dealing with more and more practical details. These details will include what must happen each week, month, and year if your church is to embrace the mission God has placed before it. In other words, you will begin implementing the plan for realizing the vision.

At this point in the revitalization process, I advise overseers to develop what I call "bifocal vision." You will need to develop the ability to simultaneously keep your eyes on the horizon and also on the terrain immediately in front of you and your church. You must maintain clarity around the destination to which God is calling your church while also tending to the close-up challenges in the execution of your ministry mission.

Especially for overseers, this can be both an exciting and a stressful time. These early steps will be the first concrete actions you will lead your church in taking as it assumes its role in fulfilling Christ's commission. But it is also here that the greatest care must be given and the greatest oversight exercised, for missteps in these early stages can have outsized consequences for the revitalization process.

Still, as the proverb reminds us, "the journey of a thousand miles begins with a single step," and you are now at the threshold of your church's journey; the step must be taken. And so, as an overseer, your task now is to lead your church in answering the fundamental question: Where do we start?

Where Do We Start?

As we have already seen, your vision must include objectives: the structural underpinnings that provide the focus and direction for each year of the church's five- to seven-year vision cycle. You have already spent prayerful time with your leadership and vision teams to develop these objectives, conscious that they must constitute the bold, church-wide efforts designed to guide your church along the path toward renewal and achievement of its God-given mission. Now it's time to integrate these objectives into your annual planning process.

Your annual plan, as the name implies, is your yearly plan for moving the church forward toward the fulfillment of the mission the Lord has placed before it. Each year of the multi-year vision cycle, you will develop and implement a new annual plan, each made up of specific objectives that the church should accomplish on the way to realization of the vision. Your annual plan will delineate the "big step" that the church will take during each year, and it will be broken down into elements that will be accomplished during the 30-, 60-, and/or 90-day increments of the year. This is how the overseer, Nehemiah, accomplished the reconstruction at Jerusalem, as recorded in Nehemiah 3. He broke the task of rebuilding the wall down into manageable, "bite-sized" parts.

To get started, you must first decide which of your objectives should be accomplished as part of your first annual plan. Overseers should consult closely with their leadership teams to decide which of the three to six objectives established as part of the vision-casting process should be implemented first.

I've found that most often, it's important for the church to build the initial objective around vision awareness and adoption. This provides the overseer and other leaders the opportunity to make sure everyone is on board before the journey begins in earnest. Overseers should not underestimate the time and care needed to ensure that the vision is deeply embedded in the consciousness of the church. In fact, I recommend that pastors should plan two sermon series dedicated to fully announcing, clarifying, and discussing the guiding vision and its biblical foundations. The first should ideally be delivered near the time of the announcement of the vision to the church. The second should follow about six months later, and in between, overseers and other church leaders should allow ample time for smaller gatherings where the vision can be explained, discussed, and most importantly, placed before God in prayer. In other words, if you're getting the idea that there should be abundant discussion around vision acceptance and adoption by the church, you're right on target!

In this connection, it's useful to take another look at Josiah, one of our biblical exemplars. Recall that his first public act, following his conviction over the sins of the nation, was to go to the temple, accompanied by "all the men of Judah and all the inhabitants of Jerusalem and the priests and the prophets, all the people, both small and great" (2 Kings 23:1,2) and to read to them the words of God's covenant. Not only that, but the king made a public vow to obey the Lord and pursue the mission of restoration that God had put on his heart. And then he took another important step that was calculated to embed the vision even more deeply in the hearts of the people.

> Then the king commanded all the people saying, "Celebrate the Passover to the LORD your God, as it is written in this book of the Covenant." Surely such a Passover had not been celebrated from the days of the judges who judged Israel, nor in all the days of the kings of Israel and of the kings of Judah. But in the eighteenth year of King Josiah this Passover was observed to the LORD in Jerusalem (2 Kings 23:21–23).

Josiah, as overseer for his nation, knew that it was vital to emphasize and repeat the vision of Judah's return to the teachings of God. He announced them himself, and then he saw to it that, year after year, the people of Jerusalem and Judah would recite and re-experience the ancient story of God's deliverance, providing repeated opportunities for the vision of the king, given to him by God, to be further ingrained into their minds and hearts.

In this connection, it's appropriate to emphasize how important shared stories can be in clarifying and imprinting the vision on the hearts and minds of people in the church. No doubt, in your preaching and teaching, you will want to incorporate stories drawn from the history of your church and its people that capture the essence of the vision and portray for your listeners what the successful achievement of the vision looks, feels, and sounds like.

For example, I know of a church that has made ministry to foster children a central part of its vision. On a regular basis, this church celebrates the victories and accomplishments of children and families they support through the program. In this way, they consistently keep before the congregation a consciousness of the people to whom they are ministering, the objectives of the ministry, and the successful outcomes that are the aim of the ministry.

Starting in the Right Place

As you and your leadership team consider which objective will constitute the first step for the church, you should ask yourselves some key questions:

◇ Which objective from our vision process will the church most easily get behind?

◇ Considering the nature of our vision, is there one objective that is the most logical "first step"?

◇ Is there a particular sequence in which we should pursue our objectives?

◇ How will our first objective help us build momentum for future plans?

◇ Is this truly a church-wide objective?

◇ Can this objective sustain the church for an entire year?

◇ Is this objective something all members can work on together?

◇ Will accomplishing this objective move the church closer to the biblical ideal?

◇ Can this objective, if achieved, be celebrated as a victory by the entire church body?

Careful consideration of these and similar questions will lead you toward the most appropriate "launch" for the church's pursuit of its God-given vision. Once you have arrived at the first objective to be accomplished, you will begin preparing to present it to the church as the first year's "big step."

What Is Our Next Step?

Now that your objective is identified, you need to drill down even farther, establishing the elements that will make up the objective. Remember: the objective identifies where you want the church to be in a year. But the elements are your plan for 30-, 60-, and 90-day increments to ensure that the objective is being achieved.

A pastor once asked me if an element could take as much as an entire year. I said to him, "If that is what it takes to accomplish the task, then yes." Remember, you are not a slave to your objectives or elements; the suggested ranges are there to serve you as you customize the process in ways to suit your church and its situation.

Because the elements are the details and outcomes necessary for the accomplishment of the objective, they need to be specific, actionable, and, most likely, measurable, since they form the "building blocks" of your annual plan. It is typical for an annual objective to be made up of four to six elements.

As you consider the elements of your annual objectives, ask yourself questions like these:

◇ How does the successful completion of this element lead toward the fulfillment of our overall goal?

◇ How is this element related to the others making up this objective? Do the elements as a whole logically support and complete the objective?

◇ How or to what degree will the accomplishment of this element be seen as a "win" for the church?

◇ How likely is it that we can complete this element within a year?

◇ Is this element actionable? How will we know when we've accomplished it?

It is vital for the overseer and the leadership team to be in sync as preparations are made to roll out the annual plan for each year of the vision cycle. I have found that most churches benefit from a "leadership summit" in which the plan, the objective for the year, and each of the elements is thoroughly discussed. The leadership summit should result in answers, agreement, and buy-in around questions like:

◇ Who needs to know that this is the plan for the church?

◇ How can we launch, explain, and unpackage this plan so that the church will enthusiastically support it?

◇ What sort of visuals or other media should we use to accurately and effectively place this plan before the church?

◇ What is the best timing for presenting this plan to the church?

◇ When should we/I preach about this plan?

◇ What are our scriptural anchors for the plan?

Refer to *Image 8* for a visual depiction of the *Annual Plan*.

Getting the leadership team on board in this way will enhance the communication process throughout the church. This also lays a good foundation for aligning small fellowship groups, Bible study groups, and other membership units in the church for understanding and buy-in. Overseers may want to incorporate special study series, Q&A sessions, and other activities to ensure that the plan is not only understood but clearly visualized and supported by all members of the church.

Why Seven Years?

Some have no doubt noticed that when we discuss the church revitalization process, we tend to speak in terms of seven-year cycles. In fact, we recommend that overseers help their churches craft an annual plan for each year of the cycle, with objectives and elements to support the achievement of each plan. But why seven years? Is there some significance in this particular span of time?

According to some researchers, there is actually a biological basis for thinking this way. They indicate that from birth to death, the human body and mind are attuned to cycles of growth, development, and change that can be categorized

(Image 8)

THE PYRAMID | Annual Plan

Now that you have identified what must be accomplished in the first "Big Step" in year one, it is time to design Side 3 of your pyramid: the *Annual Plan*.

_____'s Annual Plan is:
        (church name)

FIRST BIG STEP

_____

_____

_____

ELEMENTS OF ANNUAL PLAN

1. _____

_____

2. _____

_____

3. _____   5. _____

_____   _____

4. _____   6. _____

_____   _____

in brackets corresponding closely to each seven-year period, starting with newborn babies and extending to persons in their 80s and 90s.

But of course, there is also a biblical basis for the seven-year cycle. When God created the universe, He did it in six days and set aside the seventh day for Himself and his people as a time of rest, or "sabbath." Likewise, in Deuteronomy 15, God proclaimed every seventh year as a "sabbath year," when debts might be forgiven, enslaved persons might be freed, and the poor might be lifted up. Likewise, Joseph's visions in Genesis 41 came in seven-year cycles.

In my work with churches, I have found that the seven-year cycle lends itself to the process by allowing sufficient time for each phase to be fully implemented. For example, the first three years of the cycle often correspond to the time needed for the empowering vision to be fully incorporated and adopted throughout the church membership. Then, years four through six often mark the period during which the church achieves its greatest effectiveness in carrying out the steps of the annual plan and meeting the goals of the vision. Finally, year seven, in addition to being a time of celebrating accomplishment, often also becomes a period of looking forward to what is next for the church as it embraces its next vision. Following this pattern encourages what we at Corpus refer to as perpetual revitalization.

All this points again to the importance of developing a plan for each year of the cycle, ensuring that the particular goals and objectives of each year match with and support the progress the church is making toward achieving the vision. Each year's plan should both build on the successes of and address any shortfalls in the previous year's plan.

Maintain Flexibility

As Gen. Dwight D. Eisenhower famously said, "No plan survives contact with the enemy." Now, I recognize that overseers are certainly not dealing with "enemies" when they are engaged in the Kingdom work of leading revitalization in their churches. Nevertheless, General Eisenhower has a valid point: plans must inevitably change to match the unfolding events "on the ground." For this reason, overseers are well advised to keep an element of flexibility as they develop and implement annual plans, knowing that things change, and adaptation is necessary.

For example, I once worked with a church where the seven-year vision called for significant enhancement and changes to the physical facilities. Our original plan called for "building up" to this need during the first four years and implementing the changes to the facilities in year five. However, once we got into the process, it became evident that the church was going to be ready, financially, spiritually, and emotionally, to start construction and remodeling much earlier. Accordingly, we decided to move up the facilities phase to year three. This meant, however, that other aspects of the original plan had to be reconfigured, rescheduled, and rethought based on the earlier availability of the needed physical facilities.

Remember, it's a lot easier to change a plan that has been well thought out and carefully organized than one which exists only in the imagination of one or two individuals. In other words, good planning lends itself much more readily to flexibility and adaptation than haphazard or no planning.

Setting up the Plan

Overseers, this is a good time to recall our discussion in chapter 3 of "thinking in the presence of God." The only way that you can guide your church toward the mission God has placed before it is when you see your church clearly, both in the light of its present circumstances and in the context of the changes God is calling the church to make. As you prayerfully contemplate your church, you must seek the Lord's guidance in how you prioritize the steps of the revitalization plan.

Walk around the Church with Jesus

Take a close look at the church, both its physical facilities and its human assets, and ask Jesus the question, "What should we do for better alignment with Your commission?" Perhaps the vision Christ is placing before you entails an expanded ministry to young families in your neighborhood, or perhaps God is calling you to serve an immigrant community by offering free English classes; can your classroom and other facilities handle the increased load? If your vision involves planting churches in other communities or cities, do you need additional staff to provide remote support and liaisons with those you will commission and send out?

Too often, we assume that the Lord isn't interested in the "nitty-gritty details" of infrastructure and personnel. I believe, rather, that overseers should be placing these types of considerations before the Lord in faithful prayer, asking for insight, conviction, and spiritual imagination for any resources needed for bringing the vision to reality. Just as God empowered the Macedonian Christians to give generously in support of Paul's vision of relief for the suffering believers in Jerusalem, He can empower our churches to provide for and be stewards of His mission today. But first, dedicated overseers must clearly perceive what is needed and effectively communicate the needs to the church.

Celebrate the Victories

We all know that success breeds success. Just as this is true for sports teams and business organizations, it is true for churches embarking upon revitalization. For this reason, it's important for overseers to notice and celebrate the "wins," especially those that come early in the process. Overseers should find ways to incorporate such celebrations into sermons. Leaders may even want to designate periodic "Celebration Sundays" when certain goals have been reached, making sure that the church as a whole knows about and takes satisfaction in the successes that have been achieved. Some "easy wins" that could offer such opportunities might include increased tithing, new members, increases in small group attendance and activity, baptisms, evangelism efforts, appointment and ordination of new ministers or other leaders, and many others. Identifying and publicly celebrating such milestones can build momentum for the church's acceptance of and progress toward completion of the annual plan. This will also spur the church toward deeper spiritual growth and a more widespread embodiment of the goals and values of the empowering vision.

CHAPTER

7

Goals Make Your Vision Bloom

As a youngster, I played youth sports, and I still enjoy watching sports on TV. I especially enjoy the Summer Olympics, and I really love to watch the track and field events. There are few things more thrilling than seeing the runners in a race as they round the final curve on the track, straining toward the tape. The roar of the crowd becomes almost a physical force as the onlookers cheer for their favorite runner; the athletes are the very image of striving and determination as they give their last burst of strength, trying to be the first across the finish line.

But what if there were no finish line? What if the competitors were told, "Just go to the track and run; after a while, someone will stop you." Who would want to participate in a race with no conclusion? Who'd want to watch?

Maybe you're a fan of the NBA, or you look forward eagerly to the Final Four, at the end of the NCAA basketball season. Suppose the players came onto the court, and the hoops and nets had been removed? How could the game even happen? Why would anyone bother?

Clearly, goals are indispensable for any type of effort with any degree of importance. They are hard-wired into our human nature. In fact, one of the most insidious and dangerous symptoms of depression occurs when a person no longer believes they have anything to look forward to, to achieve, or to anticipate. The fact is that we need goals in order to thrive—or even to survive.

CHAPTER 7

How Do You Know You're Making Progress?

Occasionally, you may hear certain people say or intimate that there is something inappropriate or "un-spiritual" about goal-setting in church contexts. But the fact is that the church would not exist without goals. After all, Jesus set a clear goal for his followers when He said, "Go and make disciples of all nations." The Great Commission implies a direction, a purpose, and a desired outcome—a goal. Likewise, the early church applied their goal-setting to global evangelism: "Jerusalem, Judea, Samaria, and the uttermost parts of the earth."

Overseers who invest time and prayerful effort in developing a mission statement for their church are doing it because they envision a goal: an objective that, when reached, will indicate the achievement of an important Kingdom purpose. As long as these goals glorify God, align with His purpose, and do not violate His word, goal setting can be an important and helpful spiritual exercise.

Each of us has an innate need to know if we're headed in the right direction, and that is nowhere more important than in our spiritual lives. Both individually and collectively, followers of Jesus need goals. As an overseer involved in the church revitalization process, it is your spiritual responsibility to provide that direction for your church. Otherwise, how will your congregation know their destination or when they've arrived? As the great sage Yogi Berra once said, "If you don't know where you're going, you'll wind up somewhere else."

In other words, the goals that your church sets are among the primary evidences that you need as an overseer to answer the question that your members will inevitably ask: "Are we making a difference?" They, like all people, have an instinctive need to know whether they are on the right path and headed for the intended destination. Effective goals that are set and achieved provide the overseer the most powerful evidence to say, "Yes, we are making a difference and having an impact for the Kingdom; we can tell because we are accomplishing these goals." This evidence then becomes a powerful motivation for church members to remain as committed participants in the church revitalization effort. This is essential for building momentum!

Goals Are the Scorecard—
Both Qualitative and Quantitative

We need to be clear on three things as we begin considering the goal-setting process in the context of church revitalization. First of all, goals for the church need to be distinguished from member measures, which we'll discuss a bit later. The former are the collective accomplishments that the church body must achieve as a whole; the latter are the objectives for growth and spiritual maturity that each individual must strive for as part of the disciple-making process.

Second, overseers need to determine if setting goals annually or setting goals for the entire life of the vision is best. Many pastors have asked which is the better approach, and my answer is that either can work well; the context and approach to ministry needs to influence the way an overseer approaches goal-setting. While annual goals help you remain more flexible year to year, long-term goal setting helps you build greater momentum. During the development of your vision pyramid, the overseer, along with the vision team, should consider all these factors when determining how best to set goals.

Third, overseers will need to reflect on the differences between quantitative goals—results that can be expressed numerically—and qualitative goals—results that have more to do with attributes or values. Both types of goals are important, though they are measured and evaluated differently. Inevitably, a church will include some persons for whom quantitative goals are the most intuitive and easily understood, while other members will be more interested and attuned to qualitative goals. The overseer who truly knows and understands the church and its members will keep this in mind during the goal-setting process.

Indeed, scripture provides evidence of both quantitative and qualitative measurement during the early life of the church. In Acts 2:41 we read, "So then, those who received [Peter's] word were baptized, and that day there were added about three thousand souls." Obviously, the chronicler of the church's beginnings knew that this quantitative evidence of the power of the Gospel as preached by Peter was important to record. Later in the same chapter, we read that those who were placing their faith in Jesus had "gladness and sincerity of heart, praising God and having favor with all the people" (Acts 2:46,47). In this way, the qualitative goal of life transformation is also noted. In ways both quantitative and qualitative, the earliest Christians were making a difference and progressing toward a Great Commission goal.

In the same way, the leaders of the church who took principal responsibility for the spreading of the gospel message set goals for ministry. For example, in Romans 15,

Paul tells the Christians to whom he is writing that he has a goal to preach in Spain, where he has not yet been. He says, "I hope to see you in passing, and to be helped on my way there by you..." (Romans 15:24). Paul had a specific destination in mind, and he shared his goal of preaching in Spain with the believers in Rome to give them the opportunity to participate with him in the spreading of the gospel.

Goals Are the Outcome of Your Vision

Just as Paul's vision for proclaiming the gospel in Spain generated a goal, the vision cast by the overseer, in order to be effective, must incorporate goals that are specific in outcome and time. Such goals provide the means of harnessing natural human inclinations (the need for direction and accomplishment) to spiritual aims and purposes (the Great Commission vision for the church). Just as your strategy for the church defines the *means* for achieving the vision, the goals define the *ends*: specific accomplishments that provide the evidence for how the church is making an impact and carrying out the mission God has placed before it.

As the all-important intermediate steps toward reaching these ends—the "finish line"—goals that are properly aligned with the church's vision and mission accomplish several important things:

1. ***Goals help the church become intentional about fulfilling the Great Commission.*** When members of a church are focused on and committed to reaching a goal, they have greater clarity and direction about the work they must do to advance the Kingdom purpose.

2. ***Goals establish priorities for the church.*** When the goal is clearly defined, it is easier for members to know what aids forward progress and what hinders it. The former becomes the focus of effort; the latter is deferred or eliminated.

3. ***Goals give direction.*** When the church knows where it's headed, it is better at staying on-task and on track.

4. ***Goals provide a finish line.*** As with the examples at the beginning of this chapter, we all want to know when we've "arrived." Further, a well-defined finish line offers the opportunity for the church to celebrate accomplishments, which then catalyzes and energizes members for the next effort.

5. ***Goals keep you on-task.*** As mentioned above, when you are working toward a goal that's important to you, your desire for achievement acquires a "self-enforcing" quality that reduces distraction and propels you forward.

6. ***Goals provide motivation.*** Just as runners "strain toward the tape," we orient ourselves toward achievement. As Paul put it, "...forgetting what lies behind and straining forward to what lies ahead," we press on toward the goal (Philippians 3:13).

7. ***Goals help allocate resources.*** Just as they help us prioritize our efforts, goals help us make timely judgments about what we need and when we need it.

8. ***Goals help us make decisions.*** Bringing a vision to reality is a journey of many steps. Goals keep us focused on the steps and decisions needed *today* that keep us on course for the ultimate arrival *tomorrow*.

9. ***Goals help us know if we are making a difference.*** As mentioned previously, when goals are being reached, they provide valuable proof in the here-and-now of progress toward reaching the completion of the church's mission.

Goals are carefully and prayerfully crafted to support the church's mission, vision, and strategy; they become both the stepping-stones to success and also the validation of the ultimate outcome. Because of this, the overseer should work with the leadership team to set appropriate annual goals or goals for the five to seven years of the revitalization process. As you work with your team to develop and refine your goals, motives are very important when it comes to goal setting. I typically advise overseers to use the following questions to help refine the motive and meaning of each goal:

⋄ What goal is God leading us to achieve with this vision?

⋄ Why do we believe this goal is right for this vision?

⋄ How will the church be impacted if this goal is achieved?

⋄ How will the Kingdom of God and the community around the church be impacted if this goal were achieved?

⋄ How would God be glorified if this goal were achieved?

Methodically asking and answering these questions will lead overseers toward goals that create momentum, excitement, and deeper commitment among members as they work to help the church create and develop disciples and fulfill its part in the Great Commission.

Jim Thomas looked at his scheduler and grimaced. His next entry was, "Meet with Ella Baker." The item was no surprise; it had been on his calendar for a couple of weeks now. But it involved a conversation he was not eager to have.

Ella had been teaching in the fifth-grade Sunday School classroom at Sanford Memorial since long before Jim had answered the call to pastor this church. There were parents of college-age kids in the church who had been Ella Baker's students. Jim had heard perhaps dozens of stories about "Sister Ella" and her Bible memory drills.

But the kids who were coming to the fifth-grade classroom these days were not the same as the ones who had recited memory verses back to Ella twenty or even five years ago. Not only did these kids learn differently—a few of them even had their own smartphones—they had very little interest in the multicolored, adhesive tinfoil stars that served as Ella's "reward system" for learning all the verses for the quarterly curriculum. In fact, to hear Ella tell it, the kids had very little use for the curriculum itself. "They just won't pay attention long enough to complete the worksheets," Ella had told him, a week or so earlier.

The problem, though obvious to Pastor Jim and several of the more attentive parents, seemed beyond Ella's grasp: She was still teaching Sunday School in the 1980s, but her students lived in the third decade of the twenty-first century. So far, efforts to gently move Ella in the direction of more up-to-date instructional techniques had apparently fallen on deaf ears. "The Bible is the same today as it was a hundred years ago," she said. "And the Bible is what these children need to learn."

Jim looked at his notes for the meeting. It was imperative, if the church was going to be effective in its outreach to the community, that each member learned the importance of prioritizing others' needs over their own. For Ella Baker, that meant learning to communicate with others—especially fifth-graders—in the ways they needed, not necessarily the ways she was accustomed to using. In the margin of his scheduler, Jim had written "1 Cor 9:22: 'All things to all people...'"

There was a knock at the door. Jim stood. "Come in, Ella, and thanks for making time to see me today..."

Member Measures Change the Culture

Inevitably, institutional change comes about through personal change. Let me emphasize this by saying it another way: The greatest culture shift occurs when

CHAPTER 7

individual participants in the culture experience change. After all, institutions are made up of people, and their collective personalities, preferences, and styles blend together to create the culture that the organization presents to the rest of the world. This is true of businesses, nonprofit groups, and civic clubs. And it is certainly true of churches.

Churches Change When People Change

As an overseer, you are charged with leading the church as a collective group. But what you must always keep in mind is that ultimately, you are leading *people*. That means that you must accept responsibility for nurturing and guiding the spiritual growth and maturity of each person in the church.

Beyond its importance for the eternal destiny of each member of your church, this is urgent because of its implications for the culture of your church. As we have already discussed, the reason for the decline of many churches stems from problems with the culture: vision receptivity or the lack of it; acceptance of personal accountability for needed change; openness to new ideas; sensitivity toward the needs of others— all these and many other traits crucial to the success of the revitalization effort are functions of a church's culture. And the only way to effect meaningful change in the culture of a church is to encourage, nurture, model, and lead processes of spiritual growth and maturity in the individual members who make up the church.

Let me press this point to its extreme. The greatest threat to church revitalization is the existing culture of the church. The best way to shift the culture is to impact members' attitudes, beliefs, and behaviors.

Your Strategy and Your People

Effectively integrating member measures into your mission and strategy is the part of the process where revitalization is internalized by individual church members. The overseer must develop spiritual markers for the members of the church that will serve as tools for self-assessment and also lead individuals through a process of spiritual maturation that equips them to participate in the fulfillment of God's mission for the church.

> Member Measures are a powerful tool for shifting culture and creating unification.

(Image 9)

THE PYRAMID | Member Measures

EXAMPLE

COMPONENT 1 in the Strategy _Connect out to others_ _through service_	Essential Team Members 1. _Sam Williams_ 2. _Marsha Fields_ 3. _Devin Howard_ 4. _____ 5. _____	Member Measures 1. _Am I engaging others not like me?_ 2. _Am I sharing my story with someone this week?_
COMPONENT 2 in the Strategy _Connect in to community_ _through discipleship_	Essential Team Members 1. _Mark Wild_ 2. _Cindy O'Brien_ 3. _Tammy Light_ 4. _David West_ 5. _Ben Thompson_	Member Measures 1. _Am I taking my next step of spiritual maturity?_ 2. _Am I being transformed through the community?_
COMPONENT 3 in the Strategy _Connect up to God_ _through worship_	Essential Team Members 1. _Maria Sanchez_ 2. _Kevin Wright_ 3. _Chad Baker_ 4. _Preston Parker_ 5. _____	Member Measures 1. _Am I worshiping God daily?_ 2. _Am I being generous with all that I have?_

By creating member measures rooted in the components of the church's mission, you are putting in place your most powerful tool for shifting culture and creating unification around the multi-step strategy you must pursue in service of the vision. Keep in mind that in order to change the culture in positive ways, member measures must challenge the culture, pushing each individual member to "see beyond" the limitations currently being imposed by the existing culture.

I advise overseers and other leaders to develop member measures in a three-step process. First, select a single component of the strategy. Next, list the essential team members who will be most instrumental in carrying out the component. Finally, work with the responsible leadership team to create one or two spiritual markers that will instigate self-reflection in church members. An example of this process might involve a team in the church that will be primarily responsible for the discipleship of the members of the church (*Image 9*).

To effectively shift the culture, certain shifts in attitude and spirituality must take place in the lives of the individual members. By crafting the member measures around what is needed to achieve successful results, the overseer is not only aiding the church's progress toward the goal; he is also facilitating spiritual growth and maturity in the hearts of the individual members.

Member measures should be stated as simple, yet transformational goals that can serve as the basis for weekly or daily reflection. Ideally, they should comprise a question or two that can be answered with a qualitative description of the desired outcome.

Disciple through Announcements

Observant overseers may be able to identify multiple opportunities to reinforce and encourage individual members' growth and maturity in the ordinary course of various events and occasions in the church. One example might be as simple as incorporating member measures and goals in the regular announcements to the congregation.

By announcing and reflecting publicly on measures and goals for implementing the vision, the overseer provides opportunities for individual reflection on the part of each member. This regular reminder of the member measures and goals can lead to greater personal ownership of each member's stake in helping the church accomplish its God-given mission.

One example of this practice that I have seen used effectively in a number of churches involves focus on small group participation and personal transformation. First, participation levels are quantifiable. Also, raising up leaders of groups within the church provides opportunities for individual spiritual growth. Finally, members grow closer in fellowship and commitment through small groups. And there are many other benefits besides.

Disciple through Relationships

One of the most fundamental principles of the Christian faith is captured in 1 John 2:6: "Whoever says he abides in him ought to walk in the same way in which he walked." Remember that the concept of "walking with Jesus" implies time spent with Him: listening, observing, learning, and imitating the Great Overseer.

In the same way, overseers must "walk with" those for whom they have been given a spiritual charge. As with Pastor Jim in the earlier story, there will inevitably come times when, in the course of a relationship, words of admonition will be needed. This is an essential component of disciple-making. When the overseer observes an individual facing challenges in taking the necessary steps toward spiritual maturity, it is time to "walk alongside" them and provide guidance, teaching, encouragement, and even, sometimes, correction.

Overseers must also be able to empower and train other leaders to "walk with" those in their circles of close fellowship. Just as Paul instructed Timothy and Titus to "urge the young men to be self-controlled" and to encourage older men "as you would a father," overseers should equip leaders in the church to be mindful of the spiritual growth and maturity of those with whom they are in relationship.

It is an awe-inspiring thought to imagine what can happen when a body of believers, inspired by a vision, is striving both collectively and individually toward a God-given goal. By creating clear goals for the church, and by guiding each member toward spiritual maturity in service of those goals, overseers can catch the vision of Paul's ideal, when he described the outcome of Jesus' provision for the revitalization of the church:

> *... for the equipping of the saints for the work of service, to the building up of the body of Christ, until we all attain to the unity of the faith and of the knowledge of the Son of God, to a mature man, to the measure of the stature which belongs to the fullness of Christ... (Ephesians 4:12,13)*

Use Creativity and Passion to Drive Your Church

CHAPTER
8

Get On The Path For Discipleship

"Pastor, I'm worried about some of the kids in my group, but I don't know what to do about it." Jamal Robinson's brow furrowed as he leaned across Bob Dunbar's desk. "Attendance at the small group sessions has been pretty good, I guess, and we're getting through the discussion questions Pastor Lance provided, but..." Jamal looked down and heaved a sigh. He locked eyes with his pastor. "I don't think I'm doing a very good job of leading the group—at least, not the way I understand what we're supposed to be doing."

Bob nodded thoughtfully. Jamal was one of the most active and engaged members at Grace Community Church, which was exactly why Bob and the other ministers had invited him to be one of the hosts for the new small-group fellowship initiative. In fact, Jamal's group had been one of the first to fill up when the sign-up forms were posted on the church website. He was a teacher and coach at one of the neighborhood high schools, and many of the young people in the group Jamal hosted with his wife, Annetta, were students at his school or friends the students had invited. Just last week, in fact, Bob and Lance, the youth pastor, had been discussing the groups, and Jamal's group had come in for special commendation.

"Have you shared your concerns with Pastor Lance?" Bob asked.

Jamal nodded. "Yes. We talked and prayed over this at the

beginning of the month. But I'm just not seeing anything changing. They're good kids, and they really enjoy being together, so I guess that's a good thing, but... I was hoping to see some real changes in their lives by now. And I'm just not seeing it." Jamal leaned back in his chair and stared into the corner. "I'm thinking that maybe someone else should take the group."

Alarm bells rang out in Bob's mind. But he took a couple of deep breaths and reflected several seconds before replying. "Jamal, thank you for being open about this. I think I know enough about you to understand that this is not an easy conversation for you to have."

Jamal shook his head.

"And I want you to believe that I don't see this as any reflection on your commitment to the Lord or to this church."

"No, sir," Jamal said in a firm voice. "I just want to lead these kids to a deeper commitment to Christ. And I don't think we're getting there."

"I understand. But I wonder if, before we make any big changes in the group, you'd be willing to try one more thing?"

Jamal tilted his head questioningly. "What's that?"

"I wonder if you'd be willing to share some of what you're feeling with the kids in the group, themselves."

Surprise crossed Jamal's face. "Well... I don't want to make this about me."

"Of course, you don't. You've got a shepherd's heart, Jamal, and you're thinking about your flock—the kids in the group. But remember what Jesus told us about the shepherd and the sheep? He said the sheep hear their shepherd's voice, and they follow Him because they trust Him. Jamal, do you think you've developed a trust relationship with these kids? At least some of them?"

"Well... yes, I think so."

"Then maybe it's time for them to hear your voice. When Lance and I sat down with the other pastors to develop the discussion questions for the groups, we were aiming for a broad coverage, hoping that the questions would be a starting point for some deeper conversations. It sounds to me like it might be time for you to let the kids know about what's going on in your heart. You might be surprised what kinds of opportunities that could open up."

Jamal took a deep breath. "Well, I need to think about it and talk to Annetta."

Bob nodded. "Yes, you do. And how about if we start that process by praying about it together, right now?"

From One Step to the Next

By now, I hope that you have internalized the principle that the process of church revitalization is designed in a logical progression, starting with a foundation established on Jesus' Great Commission and proceeding in a series of steps that build upon one another. When these steps are repeated and completed, the mission should be fulfilled. Beginning with the inspiring, empowering vision that God gives to the overseer and proceeding through the various stages of discernment, mission design, objectives, and elements, overseers are leading their churches steadily toward the goal of fulfilling their church's ultimate directive. Jesus announced this directive to His followers just before His ascension: to create, nurture, and send out into the world disciples of Jesus.

As I've previously mentioned, I love the concepts presented by Jim Collins in his book, *Good to Great*. And one of the most central of these concepts is based on the ancient Greek parable of the fox and the hedgehog. As Collins retells it, the fox is a very intelligent and adaptable creature that is good at many things. By contrast, the humble hedgehog is very good at only one thing. Collins suggests that organizations—including churches—who desire to have the greatest impact would do well to emulate the hedgehog by becoming the best in the world at one thing. For the church, that one thing is disciple-making. The church must be the best in the world at disciple-making.

The early church clearly understood this. Internalizing Jesus' Great Commission as presented in Matthew 28:18–20, Mark 16:15–16, Luke 24:44–49, and John 20:19–23, the earliest Christians intentionally set about creating disciples as they became Christ's witnesses in "Jerusalem, Judea, Samaria, and the uttermost parts of the earth" (Acts 1:8).

Outflows of One Step Become Inflows of the Next

As we've also previously discussed, overseers need not wonder about the basic steps of Jesus' plan for disciple-making; he left a clear, four-step pattern for us to follow:

1. Come and see;

2. Follow me;

3. Abide in me;

4. Go and tell.

It is vital to realize that throughout this process, one step leads logically to the next. It is also essential to recognize that the results of one step become the raw materials that flow into the next step. Further, the process lends itself to infinite replication. Just as Jesus invited his first followers to come, follow, abide, and then sent them out to tell others, those disciples, in their turn, reached out to still others, teaching and empowering them to do the same. Some two thousand years later, the church still possesses this simple and repeatable pattern: the clear

(Image 10)

Come and See

Follow Me

Abide in Me

Go and Tell

Jesus' Four-Step Discipleship Model

and compelling strategy for disciple-making provided by Jesus.

> Until we recover our urgency around fulfilling the Great Commission, revitalization of churches will continue to languish.

But too often, our churches are failing to maintain disciple-making as our chief priority—our "hedgehog strategy." The church has substituted celebrity culture and programming for Jesus. Until we recover our urgency around fulfilling the Great Commission, revitalization of churches will continue to languish. And so, as we come to the path of disciple-making, we are approaching the place where "the rubber meets the road." All our previous planning, study, discernment, vision-casting, mission design, and the rest have brought us to the place where we must set the individual members of the church on the path to deeper, more committed, more meaningful discipleship. This is what Paul indicated he was laboring to achieve in Galatians 4:19 when he described himself as being "in the pains of childbirth" until Christ was formed in the Galatian disciples. As each member of the church begins to realize Paul's ideal— "Christ in you, the hope of glory" (Colossians 1:27)—the church will be transformed and revitalized, and the Great Commission will become a reality in your community.

Articulate Details to Produce Desired Results

One of the places where the revitalization process can most easily break down is when overseers fail to think carefully about how each step along the path of disciple-making should look. Too often the church has relied on programs to accomplish this work. Also, pastors and other leaders too frequently assume that leaders know what sort of guidance they should be providing, or that members know what they should be doing in order to take the next step of discipleship, or that the church knows what success in a given step looks like. Skilled overseers cannot afford to make assumptions about any of these situations!

Instead, you must give careful thought to the types of details that others will not typically consider. As you employ your top-line strategies to think about the inputs and outcomes necessary for the completion of your church's disciple-making path, you and your leadership team should carefully and prayerfully contemplate questions like these:

◇ Who needs to be involved in helping the church take this step?

◇ What kind of training or equipping do leaders need to help members take this step?

◇ What specific actions (member measures) should members be taking to complete this step?

◇ What specific outcomes will indicate successful completion of this step?

Let me emphasize this point one more time: It is the spiritual task of overseers to think through the details of each step along the path to disciple-making because they are charged by God with exercising effective spiritual oversight and leadership. Remember, there is nothing "un-spiritual" about tending to such details! Though he probably intended a slightly different meaning, the brilliant architect Mies van der Rohe said it well: "God is in the details." By guiding your leadership team and your church through each passage of the journey toward discipleship, you are serving wisely and well, effectively "equipping the saints for works of service."

God's Path Leads to God's Outcome

Overseers who have done the careful work of discernment and who have consulted with their leadership teams to develop the mission-driven strategies for executing the church's "big idea" are now ready to begin articulating their church's unique path to becoming "the best in the world" at making and growing disciples in their particular community contexts. As you formulate these vital concepts, you should also reflect on your mission statement so that you develop a strategy for clearly communicating the path to church leaders and members.

It is useful at this point to remember the importance of repetition to effective retention on the part of church members. This is one of the reasons that it's so important to have a clear, memorable mission statement and also a brief tagline. This principle also points to the importance of providing clear visual representations of the path. By engaging "both sides of the brain" with your communication of the path, you improve your members' ability to understand, articulate, and, ultimately, follow the path to disciple-making that is central to your church's fulfillment of the Great Commission.

There are many ways to effectively communicate and represent God's path for your church. Following are some examples from churches that have applied these principles successfully *(Images 11 and 12):*

(Image 11)

spiritual formation grid

discipleship
evangelism
pathway

up through worship
out through service
in through discipleship

one discipleship culture

invest, invite, include

i^3 invest, invite, include

invest
Meaningful Relationships

invite
Worship Services

include
Small Group Communities

one discipleship culture

spiritual formation grid

WHO GOD IS	WHAT GOD DOES	WHO I AM	WHAT I DO
Creator	Calls	Redeemed	Know & Obey
Father	Adopts	Family	Love & Worship
Savior	Transforms	Member	Give & Share
Lord	Sends	Missionary	Go & Multiply

5 Elements of Discipleship

• Cultivate meaningful relationships
• Engaging in biblical learning
• Praying and caring for each other
• Living together on God's mission
• Developing new leaders

(Image 12)

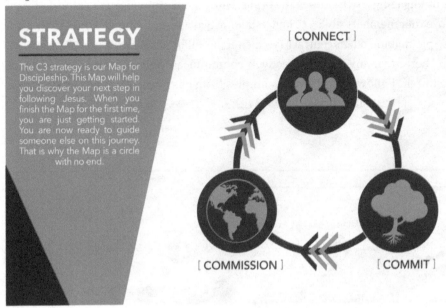

STRATEGY

The C3 strategy is our Map for Discipleship. This Map will help you discover your next step in following Jesus. When you finish the Map for the first time, you are just getting started. You are now ready to guide someone else on this journey. That is why the Map is a circle with no end.

[CONNECT]

[COMMISSION]

[COMMIT]

As overseers consider their particular communities and the needs, passions, capabilities, and resources available to their own churches, they should develop their own individual expressions of the disciple-making path that will best communicate with their members. Keep in mind that, though it is important to have a statement and visual representation for your path that is memorable, you must go beyond slogans and catchphrases to develop detailed expressions of each step along the path so that leaders and members will know what they should be doing. The point is not to have the most creative and eye-catching graphics—though that can be very helpful. Rather, the point is to provide as much clarity as possible about each step in the process and what activity it should include while describing the desired outcome. Once this process is designed to achieve the necessary outcome, the goal is to have it impact as many people as possible.

Culture Is Mission-Critical

As we have already shared, the culture of any organization is the sum of the individual qualities of its people. When Jesus looked at the seven churches of Asia in Revelation 2 and 3, he saw how the collective attitudes, actions, perceptions, and motivations of each of the churches were being manifested in that church's expression of faithfulness—or the lack of it—to the Great Commission.

It bears repeating: The number-one reason that churches are in decline is because their culture has lost its focus on making and growing disciples of Christ. When the church becomes dedicated to any other end, it ceases to carry out its primary Kingdom mission. It follows, then, that overseers who want to successfully lead their churches through the revitalization process must dedicate themselves to planting, nurturing, and propagating a culture of disciple-making.

All this explains why, starting with the earliest stages of assessment, the revitalization process asks overseers to dig deeply into questions of culture within their churches, probing attitudes of leaders and members on matters such as ministry priorities, spiritual practices, church leadership and programs, and the priorities of the members. To be effective, overseers must start from a place of accurate knowledge about the culture—the attitudes, beliefs and behaviors, and customs—of those they lead. And then they must design and lead their churches to develop a path of effective disciple-making in light of the challenges of its existing culture.

Internal Culture

Not surprisingly, church culture is often largely a function of membership culture. And for many churches, the membership exerts influence over large portions of the church. Overseers must be intimately aware of the nuances of individual members' attitudes and attributes, as these will determine the steps necessary for moving the church as a whole along the disciple-making path. For this reason, assessing the degree of vision receptivity possessed by the church membership as a whole is another one of the essential early steps in the process of discernment for church revitalization.

Attitude
+
Belief & Behavior
+
Customs
=
Internal Culture

As an overseer, by assessing matters like —

◇ membership awareness of church ministries and their importance,

◇ amount of time members spend in prayer for the church and its ministries,

◇ willingness to take steps of faith,

◇ degree of trust members place in church leadership,

◇ individual acceptance of responsibility/ownership for ministry outcomes,

◇ trust in the church's leadership vision

— and other factors, you are placing yourself in a realistic position to design steps in your path to discipleship that can actually effect positive change on an individual level.

For example, if the overseer's assessment of the church's cultural disposition toward dealing with dissension or disagreement among members reveals a tendency toward ineffective handling of conflict, it will be vital for the disciple-making path to address this. The overseer will want to incorporate specific steps that will lead members to "maintain the unity of the Spirit in the bond of peace" (Ephesians 4:3). By providing a clear path to greater spiritual maturity in dealing with disagreement, the overseer will also encourage growth in the body of Christ, equipping each member to be an agent of peace and healing, not only within the church but also in a world desperately in need of both.

If trust in leadership or lack of that trust among members is a cultural issue, then the overseer must design a path to discipleship that trains and encourages members toward greater faith and belief while nurturing and developing deeper, more trusting relationships. In this way, the faithful overseer will lead the church toward being "knit together in love" (Colossians 2:2), better equipping it to be a light to the surrounding community.

External Culture

Of course, we also know that culture doesn't end at the walls of the church. Because we are called to be "in the world," the church must be aware "of the world" to be effective witnesses to the call and mission of Jesus.

One of the key tasks of overseers who are leading church revitalization is understanding the community context in which the church exists. This encompasses community history, demographics, interests, and attitudes, along with your community's story. These factors influence the attitudes, beliefs and behaviors, and customs of the community. All of these influences can, to some degree, blind Christians to the challenges of their own maturity, which underlines once again the importance of developing effective member measures, as mentioned in chapter 7. To continue the process of making and growing disciples of Jesus in your community, the church must be effective in knowing how to encourage unbelievers. And in order for your church to develop effective outreach to your community, the members and leadership require an understanding of the community's culture. Just as with the disciple-making process within the church, effective outreach starts with a recognition of where people are and then invites them to take steps toward where the Lord desires for them to be.

> Overseers who are leading church revitalization need to understand the community context in which the church exists.

The next step will be designed to teach and model for them how a disciple thinks, believes, and behaves. Finally, the church should think through how the existing community culture influences the way in which it sends disciples to serve others and the world.

Cultural Assessment and Your Path

Perceptive overseers will have realized by now that so much of the success of the church revitalization process goes back to the two words spoken by Jesus to each of the seven churches of Asia: "I know." In our discussion of the *Convergence*, we noticed that in order for overseers to find the place where passion, purpose, community, and potential intersect with the God-given mission, they must know their church on a granular level. Only with such a clear-eyed assessment in hand can overseers and other leaders discern the steps needed for the church to fulfill its mission of disciple-making.

Replacing Bad Culture with Good

When Jesus gave direction to the seven churches of Asia, he told them clearly which aspects of their culture had to change in order for them to return to the path of effective disciple-making. It is the same today for overseers who are leading their churches toward revitalization. Members need to know the concrete steps they must take for objectives to be met. They must know, on a person-to-person level, what behaviors and spiritual attributes will lead to greater maturity.

As we discussed at the end of chapter 7, designing and implementing effective member measures will change the culture by shifting the attitudes, beliefs, and behaviors of existing church members. Overseers should also seek to cultivate and develop the member measures in new disciples as they, in turn, help to create the new culture needed for revitalization.

In a later chapter, we'll discuss more details of the group dynamics surrounding cultural change, but for now, suffice it to say that in any group, various people will receive and accept changes in the culture at different times and with different levels of enthusiasm. Some of this difference depends on the reasons and the degree to which they are attached to the current culture, and in some cases, certain individuals may prove intractable in their negative attitudes toward the changes needed to create a culture of discipleship. It is the task of an overseer to recognize these different types of people and engage with them in appropriate, spiritually mature ways.

Note, though, that the overseer cannot do all the work with challenging members. Eventually, other members must take up the responsibility to contend for the specific and clear plan for making and sending disciples. The goal, of course, is to bring about the positive changes in the culture—and each individual member—that are necessary for revitalization to succeed.

Nehemiah Leads and Protects Cultural Change

When we last saw Nehemiah, he had traveled to Jerusalem, performed a detailed assessment of the work needed to rebuild the walls of the city, and confronted the naysayers Sanballat, Tobiah, and Geshem. As a skilled and perceptive overseer, Nehemiah also set about leading cultural change, shifting the attitudes of his followers from dismay at the magnitude of the task to a desire to get the work underway.

A little later on, scripture provides us with another telling interlude depicting the ways in which an overseer must not only promote but also safeguard the cultural change that is needed for the mission to succeed. We'll pick up the story as the work on the wall is well underway, with various groups taking responsibility for rebuilding sections of the wall. Reading Nehemiah's account of the rebuilding, it is almost amusing when we reach Nehemiah 4:6, where it is written, "So we built up the wall. And all the wall was joined together to half its height, for the people had a mind to work." Indeed they did!

But as we have already noted, cultural change of the type needed to carry out God's mission will almost always engender opposition. This was certainly true in Nehemiah's case. Notice what happens in the very next verse:

> Now when Sanballat, Tobiah, the Arabs, the Ammonites, and the Ashdodites heard that the repair of the walls of Jerusalem went on, and that the breaches began to be closed, they were very angry. All of them conspired together to come and fight against Jerusalem and to cause a disturbance in it. But we prayed to our God, and because of them we set up a guard against them, day and night (Nehemiah 4:7–9).

Scripture goes on to record that Nehemiah and the other leaders with him organized the work parties so that some would attend to repairing the wall while others stood ready, armed and on guard against any threat. Workers labored with a trowel in one hand and a spear in the other; each man toiled "with his sword strapped to his side as he built."

Nehemiah, in other words, led a cultural shift from one of willingness to begin the work to one of readiness to protect the progress of the work. Recognizing that opposition to the God-appointed mission was inevitable, he took steps to ensure that the people knew what changes in behavior were necessary to guard against the threat.

In the same way, overseers must remain vigilant against obstacles and threats to the ongoing work of disciple-making and individual spiritual growth. Sometimes the opposition will come from outside. Perhaps more often, it will arise from within, as those who were comfortable with "the way things were" seek to disrupt, delay, or avoid the church's progress toward fulfilling its mission.

CHAPTER 8

A faithful overseer, led by the Holy Spirit and under the conviction of the call of Jesus, has the responsibility to perceive and mitigate these threats. In doing so, the overseer will steady the hands of those he leads to continue their work. He will keep their feet on the path toward deeper, more committed discipleship.

9

Create Your Leadership Ladder

When we look at the biblical record concerning the visionary leaders raised up by God to accomplish renewal among his people, one of the things we notice is that God's vision, once implanted in a human heart, soon outgrows its source. In every case, the vision draws others unto itself, as God's spirit moves among His people, inspiring and empowering.

In fact, we can see this principle at work in each of the three exemplary biblical overseers we've discussed so far. When Joseph was raised up by God to save the nation of Egypt—and, ultimately, the founding fathers of Israel—from a seven-year famine, one of the first things he did was to go "through all the land of Egypt" (Genesis 41:46) in order to put in place the organization and subsidiary leadership necessary to organize such a massive effort. King Josiah, pierced to the heart over the wickedness of his nation that had brought upon it the wrath of God, called to himself "all the elders of Judah and Jerusalem" and "all the men of Judah and all the inhabitants of Jerusalem and the priests and the prophets" (2 Kings 23:1,2) to impart the urgency of his vision for the spiritual renewal of the nation. And certainly, we can identify the ways in which Nehemiah distributed responsibility and leadership for rebuilding and defending the various sections of the ruined walls of Jerusalem as he appointed clans, groups from various communities, and even members of the priesthood to take charge of portions of the task (Nehemiah 3).

This same principle is easily observed in the earliest days of the church, as the apostles directed the ordination of deacons who could oversee the important work of administering the distribution of food to those in need. And we see it in even greater detail in the work of the apostle Paul, both as he directed Timothy and Titus to appoint spiritual leaders in all the churches, and specifically in his careful provision for the church in Philippi.

A Leadership Plan Is Essential

As Paul considered this church, which he had personally planted during his second missionary journey, he had some very specific thoughts about the type of leadership required to help the Philippian Christians continue in their faith and witness. He wrote to them:

> *I hope in the Lord Jesus to send Timothy to you shortly, so that I also may be encouraged when I learn of your condition. For I have no one else of kindred spirit who will genuinely be concerned for your welfare. For they all seek after their own interests, not those of Christ Jesus. But you know of his proven worth, that he served with me in the furtherance of the gospel like a child serving his father. Therefore I hope to send him immediately, as soon as I see how things go with me. And I trust in the Lord that I myself will be coming shortly. But I thought it necessary to send to you Epaphroditus, my brother and fellow worker and fellow soldier, who is also your messenger and minister to my need; because he was longing for you all and was distressed because you had heard that he was sick. For indeed he was sick to the point of death, but God had mercy on him, and not on him only but also on me, to spare me sorrow upon sorrow. Therefore I am all the more eager to send him, so that I would not have sorrow upon sorrow. Receive him then in the Lord with all joy, and hold men like him in high regard; because he came close to death for the work of Christ, risking his life to complete what was deficient in your service to me (Philippians 2:19–30).*

Paul knows that he cannot be consistently physically present with his beloved Philippians and that they will need others who can be with them and who can continue to guide their growth in discipleship. For this reason, he references a three-part spiritual leadership ladder that he intends to provide in order to ensure the type of leadership needed by the church. The three "steps" in the ladder begin with Paul, in his apostolic role, and continue with Timothy, whom Paul entrusts with the oversight of the Philippian church because he "has genuine concern" for the welfare of the church. The third step in the ladder is embodied by Epaphroditus, who "longs for" the church and also desires what is best for it.

In this intimate passage, we also get a glimpse of three important attributes of the type of leadership God desires for his people. First, Paul shares insights into the heart of a spiritual leader. Next, he offers understanding of the habits of spiritual leaders. And finally, he describes the honor that is due such faithful leaders.

The Heart of a Leader

By way of explaining why he wants to send Timothy as an overseer for the Philippian church, Paul describes the key attributes of the heart of a spiritual leader:

◇ The leader is concerned for others (v. 20);

◇ The leader safeguards the interests of Christ (v. 21);

◇ The leader is loyal (v. 22);

◇ The leader advances the gospel (v. 22).

Because Timothy's work as a spiritual leader proceeds out of a heart displaying these four attributes, Paul has confidence in giving him the oversight of the church in Philippi. And today, as overseers seek to bring about the revitalization of their churches, they should earnestly and prayerfully seek these same qualities, not only in themselves, but also in those to whom they entrust positions of leadership in their churches.

The Habits of a Leader

As Jesus said, "What comes out of the mouth proceeds from the heart" (Matthew 15:18). In the same way, the heart of a spiritual leader produces certain habits that help to ensure effectiveness as the church fulfills the Great Commission.

1. Spiritual leaders are loyal (v. 25, "my brother");

2. Spiritual leaders have a strong work ethic (v. 25, "my co-worker");

3. Spiritual leaders communicate effectively (v. 25, "your messenger");

4. Spiritual leaders care for others (v. 25, "whom you sent to take care of my needs").

Paul knows that Epaphroditus will serve the church with dedication because he has observed these "habits of the heart" in this cherished fellow believer. In the same way, overseers should seek the leading of the Holy Spirit as they raise up leaders in their churches who can both lead with vision and serve with faith and determination.

Honoring Our Leaders

Paul wisely underlines the importance of appropriately honoring spiritual leaders who serve faithfully and well. In fact, overseers are well-advised to intentionally incorporate a tradition of honoring leadership and even to embed it into the church's culture, to the degree possible. From Paul we learn that:

◇ We should rejoice in spiritual leaders (v. 28);

◇ We should receive spiritual leaders with gladness (v. 29);

◇ We should honor the risks spiritual leaders take on our behalf (v. 30).

By making special times and occasions to appropriately honor the spiritual leaders God raises up, overseers can also create greater awareness in the church of the importance of spiritual leaders who possess the qualities of heart and habits that are required to keep the church on the path of discipleship and renewal.

Paul's prescription for leadership development cannot go unnoticed. It is one of the surest ways to leave a lasting legacy and have an impact beyond your own limitations.

A Leadership Ladder for the Church

In Paul's plan for the Philippian Christians, we may perceive a relatively simple, three-step leadership ladder: 1) Paul, the apostle, or chief overseer; 2) Timothy, the "elder," or more experienced leader; and 3) Epaphroditus, the "deacon," who is stepping into a leadership role for perhaps the first time. This makes sense, as the church in Philippi was likely still at an early stage of growth, meaning that its leadership needs were still relatively simple.

It's important to recognize that the leadership pattern and the structural complexity of the leadership ladder will be governed by the size and specific needs of the church. For small churches (membership of 100 or less, with perhaps only a single pastor), a simple, three-step ladder is often all that is needed. For slightly larger churches (500 or less), a leadership ladder may need to include as many as five levels. For large churches (1,000 or more members and typically several pastors and other ministers on staff), the leadership ladder may have as many as seven different "rungs" or levels of leadership development. The point is that each overseer, in consultation with the leadership team, should decide what is right for their church, based on their knowledge of the church, its culture, its size, and its needs.

Overseers should also "customize" the leadership ladder for their church, using the terms, language, and attributes that best communicate with the members and other leaders. In other words, the leadership ladder should arise out of the church's "pyramid": its mission, values, strategy, vision, annual plan, and goals. Each step on the ladder should be intentionally designed to produce the type of leaders needed by the church to carry out its unique mission for achieving the Great Commission in your community context. As the overseer and the leadership team make decisions about the ladder's design, the order in which the various leadership development strategies will be implemented, and the specific qualities the church requires in its leaders, they are putting in place the means of building a leadership system that will "equip the saints" to make, grow, and send out disciples of Jesus.

Biblical Principles

Overseers can be confident that they are nurturing leadership qualities with a sound biblical basis. In addition to the attributes discussed in Paul's letter to the Philippians, there is a great deal of biblical guidance available for discerning the characteristics desirable in spiritual leaders. For example, a reading of Proverbs 14 reveals the following nine traits:

1. Self-control (vs. 1–3)

2. Hard-working (v. 4)

3. Knowledgeable (vs. 5–7)

4. Visionary (vs. 8–15)

5. Mature (vs. 16–17)

6. Caring (vs. 18–24)

7. Honest (v. 25)

8. Inspiring (vs. 26,27)

9. Courageous (vs. 28–35)

The Bible is filled with lists of qualities found in leaders who effectively impact God's people as they fulfill God's mission. The overseer's task is to identify and develop leaders with the necessary qualities to lead the church in fulfillment of its mission.

Perhaps not surprisingly, several of these leadership qualities overlap with those indicated in Paul's descriptions of Timothy and Epaphroditus. In fact, it is significant that Paul's discussion of his plans for sending Timothy and Epaphroditus to guide the church in Philippi occurs not long after his eloquent exhortation to the church to "Do nothing from selfish ambition or conceit" and to "count others more significant than yourselves" (Philippians 2:3); to "look to the interests of others" (Philippians 2:4) and, above all, to take on "the mind of Christ," who "emptied himself, taking on the form of a servant" (Philippians 2:7). Paul is very clear that the type of leaders—and disciples—that are needed are those who are living their lives in imitation of Christ.

Leadership Development Produces Growth

As overseers seek to right-size their leadership ladders and tailor them specifically to the needs of their churches, they must always be keeping in mind that nurturing and developing leaders is an essential part of the plan for church renewal. Only by raising up and training the type of leaders who are exactly suited and properly equipped to advance your church's mission, strategy, and goals can you successfully achieve the realization of your church's unique vision. This means, among other things, that overseers will need to carefully consider the desired outcomes of each level of leadership training in their churches. They will need to evaluate the readiness of leaders-in-training by testing them before they move to the next level. They will need to develop tools for evaluating the leaders throughout the church, and they will also require efficient tools for training the leaders as they grow and mature.

The Right Fit for Each Purpose

As mentioned before, in smaller churches, the leadership path may look more like a ribbon with three levels (*Image 13*): individual members using their gifts and talents; leaders of individuals and teams who are accomplishing essential ministry tasks; and those who provide leadership and direction to the church as a whole, helping it to achieve the mission and realize the vision.

(Image 13)

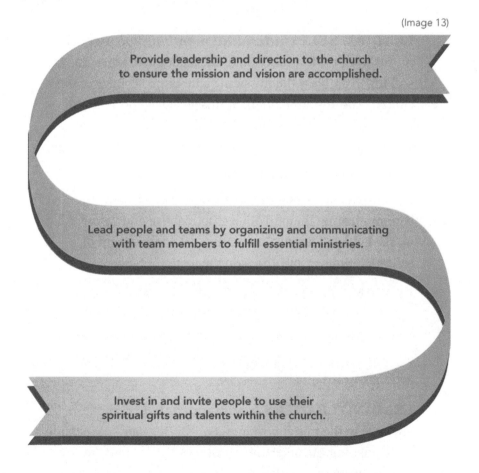

Provide leadership and direction to the church to ensure the mission and vision are accomplished.

Lead people and teams by organizing and communicating with team members to fulfill essential ministries.

Invest in and invite people to use their spiritual gifts and talents within the church.

But a leadership ladder may also encompass much more, starting at the most basic level of individual member or volunteer and proceeding all the way to those who are providing leadership in a more Kingdom-wide sense, encompassing issues that may concern the entire Body of Christ. A part of the overseer's judgment of "right fit" is to know when a leader in training is ready to be promoted to the next level. We refer to this as the "key adjustment." In order to avoid the Peter Principle (persons rising to the level of their incompetence and remaining there), the overseer will need to give attention to what characteristics should be present *before* a leader advances to the next level of leadership. Even if the model is simple, it is essential to have a leadership development plan in place as a part of the church revitalization process.

Key functions of leaders at various levels might include but are not limited to the following:

1. **LEADING SELF** *(individual member/volunteer)*— At this level the key function of the leader is to know and be seeking to embody the mission, values, and strategy of the church. The key adjustment at this level is to progress to thinking about others and helping them to do the same.

2. **LEADING OTHERS** *(team leader)*—Those who are leading others have progressed to the next level, which involves living out the mission, values, and strategy by communicating them to others, both above and below on the ladder. They are facilitating the achievement of essential ministry by others on the team.

3. **LEADING TEAMS** *(coach)*—At this level, the coach functions to identify and inspire other leaders and teams with the mission, values, and strategy. Their key adjustment is to become strategic in their thinking and actions toward others.

4. **LEADING LEADERS** *(coordinator)*—Coordinators are loyal to the mission, values, and strategy and have made the adjustment to allocating resources to facilitate the work of other leaders.

5. **LEADING DIVISIONS** *(strategist)*—Leaders at this level have begun to drive the mission, values, and strategy by developing and implementing vision and leading the culture.

6. **LEADING MINISTRY** *(church catalyst)*—These leaders provide direction for the church as a whole: developing, communicating, and inspiring the church with mission, vision, values, and strategy.

7. **LEADING IN THE KINGDOM**—At this level, the leader is involved with addressing universal issues in the broader Body of Christ, offering credible leadership that is rooted in unquestioned character. They may be locally stationed, but they are Kingdom-oriented.

Though not every leader will (or should) rise through all of the categories or levels on the church's leadership development plan, the same principles should be applied at each level. At every step along the way, the overseer must have a grasp of the essential elements needed for successful leaders of the particular church and see that they are being incorporated into the lives and ministries of the leaders. Ensuring this also ensures growth and maturity in the leaders being developed and those within their sphere of influence. This applies equally, whether we are talking about small group leaders, deacons, elders, or ministry staff. When the leadership ladder is designed to produce the type of leaders the church needs to accomplish the mission, there will be a consistency of approach up and down the ladder that will lend itself to the church's progress toward its fulfillment of the Great Commission in the community. This will create a leadership culture in the church where healthy leaders are reproduced. Also, this will cultivate good chemistry and will exert a positive impact on the overall culture of the church.

As they develop the leadership ladder for the church, overseers and those on the leadership team should be asking questions like these:

◊ What *character traits* are we looking for in our leaders?

◊ What *competencies and skills* should our leaders exhibit?

◇ What kind of *chemistry* with the ministry team and the members at large should our leaders have?

◇ What types of *concern* for the mission should our leaders display?

Refer to the template (*Image 14*) to visulaize how a 4-level *Leadership Ladder* might be developed.

At the same time these questions are being asked, overseers and the leadership team should also be evaluating the exact position on the leadership ladder where each of these considerations should occur. Additionally, they must consider how to determine when leaders in development are ready to make the transition to the next level.

These considerations, of course, must be occurring in the context of the church's culture and in service of its mission, values, vision, annual plan, and goals. Only by addressing the church's leadership needs in light of these greater aims can churches achieve the type of synergistic disciple-making that leads to revitalization.

Ken Perry waited while Margie Roberson turned over his question in her mind. He knew she wasn't entirely surprised by his request, but he also knew her well enough to anticipate that her answer wouldn't be hastily given. Finally, she looked back at him.

"What makes you think I'm the right one to lead the stewardship campaign?" she asked.

"Well, there's the obvious fact that you've acquired a well-deserved reputation in our community for being good with money."

"An occupational hazard," she said with a little smile.

"But beyond that, Margie, no one at Gilead Bible Church questions your loyalty to what we're about here. Ever since we made the commitment to give sacrificially for the church plant in Sudan, you've been a key voice, both among the deacons and with the rest of

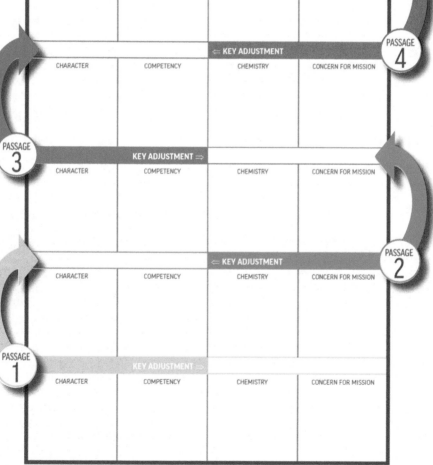

(Image 14)

THE LADDER | Develop a Custom Leadership Ladder

leadershipladder

CHARACTER	COMPETENCY	CHEMISTRY	CONCERN FOR MISSION

⇐ KEY ADJUSTMENT — PASSAGE 4

CHARACTER	COMPETENCY	CHEMISTRY	CONCERN FOR MISSION

KEY ADJUSTMENT ⇒ — PASSAGE 3

CHARACTER	COMPETENCY	CHEMISTRY	CONCERN FOR MISSION

⇐ KEY ADJUSTMENT — PASSAGE 2

CHARACTER	COMPETENCY	CHEMISTRY	CONCERN FOR MISSION

KEY ADJUSTMENT ⇒ — PASSAGE 1

CHARACTER	COMPETENCY	CHEMISTRY	CONCERN FOR MISSION

the members, supporting the importance of taking the gospel to hard places."

Margie shrugged. "Your sermon on Jonah was pretty convicting. God loves even the people we think are our enemies. You convinced me."

Ken smiled. "I'm glad. And now I want you to take the next step in that conviction and lead the church in our next big move of faith. I believe that God really wants to multiply our efforts in Sudan, but we've got to be all in. Will you help me bring the rest of the church closer to that same commitment you're feeling?"

Margie sighed. "I can see that this is what we have to do. My heart is telling me you're right. And if we stop trusting in God and only plan based on what we can see, that's not really faith, is it?"

"No, it's not. But Margie, make no mistake: this won't be easy. Some are already questioning the wisdom of our church taking on a task like this. They haven't bought into the vision yet. Part of what I'm asking you to do is accept responsibility for bringing along some folks who may not be ready to make the commitment we're asking for."

She nodded. "I understand." She shook her head and smiled. "I don't see any way around it." She looked at him. "I'm in. What do we need to do next?"

10

The Tools You Need

I have a friend who was once an avid golfer. Perhaps his "former" status is explained by his favorite definition of the game of golf, as he once shared it with me: "Golf is a sport in which the object is to place a small, white ball into a distant, slightly larger hole, using implements that are completely unsuited for the purpose." Anyone who has ever sliced a drive into the dense forest at the edge of a fairway, or watched a flubbed chip shot dribble into a greenside bunker, can probably relate to my friend's description!

Know What You Need for the Journey

In most endeavors, having the proper tools for the job is vital. Just as you wouldn't entrust a person with no medical training to perform surgery on a loved one, just as you wouldn't take your car to a mechanic who had only pliers and a few screwdrivers, you must, as an overseer leading church revitalization, have in your "toolkit" the proper resources and tools for the journey on which you are leading your church. Having these tools is required if you are to lead competently.

Furthermore, you should expect that your toolkit will be unique to your church, your pastoral style, the abilities, characteristics, and personalities of your leadership team, and, above all, the culture of your church and the vision you are pursuing. Proceeding from Jesus' imperative to "make disciples of all nations," your tools must be fitted to the specific needs of your God-given vision, mission, and goals.

In fact, the problem with many approaches to "church growth" or similar programs is that they take an "off-the-shelf" approach to the challenges facing the overseer. When you stop to think about it, how much sense does it make that the techniques and strategies suitable for an urban megachurch with ten pastors would work just as well for a small, rural congregation with a ministry staff of one? Certainly, both churches should aim to impact their communities by making, growing, and sending committed disciples, but how likely is it that what is necessary to lead one church is the same as what is necessary to lead another church?

For this reason, the approach described in the *ReFocus* process is built upon discovering the church's current realities, spiritually discerning the convergence of the church, community, and leadership, and then developing the church's directional answers to the vision questions. The *ReFocus* approach next helps you develop the plan for making disciples and building leaders. And finally, you learn how to execute effectively every day, once these elements are all discovered and in place. The reality is that none of the previous work matters if the execution does not take place or if it is ineffective. The vision must shift from being a dream to becoming a possibility. To realize the dream, execution is required. This, in turn, requires having the right tools in your toolkit and using them in the right way.

Create, Nurture, and Guard a New Culture

As we have previously discussed in various ways, the culture of a church—or almost any other group—is more powerful than vision and strategy combined. As we've also mentioned, problematic culture is typically the number-one contributor to church decline. When the church culture contains elements that threaten the disciple-making process, decline will become inevitable.

As an overseer leading church revitalization, your focus must be on developing and wisely employing the right tools to envision, articulate, and lead the cultural changes in your church that are needed to ensure disciple-making as the unifying principle. You should expect to spend more time on challenging the culture and leading cultural change than any other effort when leading in a revitalization. In fact, in your execution, everything we have discussed so far—articulating a vision, announcing a mission, communicating values, developing a strategy, crafting goals and annual plans, and all the rest—may be seen as contributing to the ultimate aim of developing a "Great Commission culture" in your church as you partner with God in the spiritual process of leading members to greater faith and more closely following Jesus.

Vision Receptivity

Few cultural aspects of your church are more important for the revitalization process—or more indicative of the likelihood of its success—than vision receptivity. If the members of the church are fundamentally unable to understand and receive the vision—or unwilling to embrace it—the overseer will find it exceedingly difficult, if not impossible, to gain the necessary traction for moving forward.

Utilizing the *Vision Receptivity Assessment* (VRA) can help overseers understand the climate for the church's readiness to accept the vision, along with the challenges and adaptations needed to move the culture in the direction of the vision. This instrument consists of a series of statements about attitudes, behaviors, and characteristics of church members and leadership that will allow you to gauge the church on a continuum that indicates the level of readiness to accept the vision, contrasted with the level of unwillingness to accept the vision. To use the VRA tools, you will score answers to questions on a scale from 1 to 10, with 1 indicating the lowest responsivity and 10 indicating the highest. The instruments cover nine different categories of church culture:

1. On Mission vs. Religious Activity

2. Courage vs. Fear

3. Trust vs. Distrust

4. Authentic Communication vs. Withheld Information

5. Clarity vs. Chaos

6. Adaptive vs. Inflexible

7. Joyful vs. Negative

8. Empowering vs. Controlling

9. Honesty vs. Deception

When you have collected the results of this assessment and scored it, you will be able to chart a graphic representation of your church's VRA to more easily visualize the cultural climate with respect to vision acceptance vs. vision rejection. Completed graphs might look something like *Image 15*:

(Image 15)

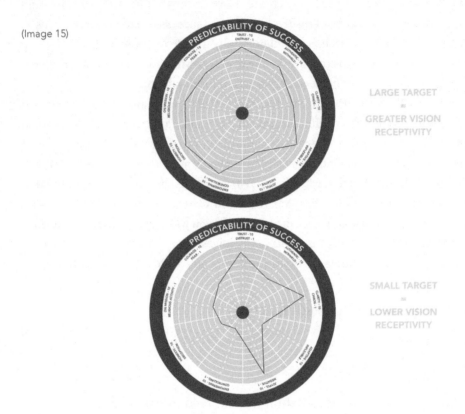

LARGE TARGET
=
GREATER VISION
RECEPTIVITY

SMALL TARGET
=
LOWER VISION
RECEPTIVITY

The larger the area encircled by the line corresponding to your results on the survey instruments, the greater your church's receptivity for the vision. The smaller the area, the lesser its receptivity.

A portion of this assessment instrument is provided in the APPENDIX at the end of this book. To learn more about the assessment tools, scan the QR Code.

Understanding Where Your Members Are

An important principle in leading cultural change for the church is understanding the basic principle that various individuals occupy various positions in the acceptance process, depending on their basic disposition toward change and the process and pace of vision adoption. Generally, people fall into one of four categories:

1. **INNOVATORS AND EARLY ADOPTERS** tend to be key leaders in the church who easily recognize the benefits of the revitalization vision. They typically see the vision as needed by the church in order to unify around and embrace a bigger and better future.

2. **MIDDLE ADOPTERS** are receptive to the new vision, but they need more questions answered before they can completely get on board. Because of this attribute, the second year of the vision adoption process is often more difficult for them than the first and is usually focused on educating them as members.

3. **LATE ADOPTERS** face their greatest challenge in year three of the process, as they grieve over what they now realize they must give up to fully support and move forward with the vision. Overseers and other leaders will typically need to engage thoughtfully and respectfully with late adopters to encourage them to release any remaining resistance and commit fully to participating in the vision. Late adopters typically need to grieve the sense of loss that comes with a new vision.

4. **NEVER-ADOPTERS AND ANTI-ADOPTERS** are resistant to the end. Never-adopters will often frame their resistance silently or passively, while anti-adopters are typically more vocal in their opposition. Overseers and other leaders must engage these individuals, giving them

opportunities to understand that the vision will be enacted and that necessary changes will be made. This will involve difficult conversations and possibly even church discipline, but if this is not done, anti-adopters will actively recruit never-adopters to form a coalition with the potential to derail church revitalization.

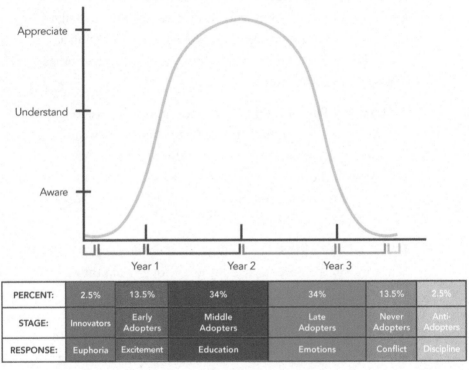

PERCENT:	2.5%	13.5%	34%	34%	13.5%	2.5%
STAGE:	Innovators	Early Adopters	Middle Adopters	Late Adopters	Never Adopters	Anti-Adopters
RESPONSE:	Euphoria	Excitement	Education	Emotions	Conflict	Discipline

(Image 16)

The thoughtful overseer will understand and anticipate the needs (and identities) of members in each of these four groups and will work with others on the leadership team to develop biblical, sensitive, and Spirit-led plans for aiding their understanding, acceptance, and participation in the vision adoption process.

Celebrating Victories and Building Momentum

Just as well-equipped overseers develop specific tools for leading change in the church culture, they also prepare needed resources for helping the church recognize and celebrate key milestones and successes on the way to mission accomplishment.

I've already mentioned a church I know of that promotes its ministry to foster children through the use of special announcements and updates celebrating accomplishments and important occasions for those in the ministry. As the church makes progress and achieves goals on the way toward accomplishing the mission, overseers, and leaders should record and find ways to celebrate the achievements with staff and membership. It is vital for the church to recognize and rejoice when ministry is being successfully carried out, especially early in the revitalization process, when building momentum and enthusiasm is so important. Overseers should give careful thought to the best formats, methods, and times for facilitating these celebrations.

Image 17

Culture

Strategy

Staff
Loyalty
(100%)

Leadership Leading (75%)

Members living the culture (51%)

Values

Mission

Celebration-worthy events might include the inauguration of a realigned worship format, attendance increases, an upward trend in baptisms, successful formation of small groups, completed evangelism outreaches, and others. Sharing stories and images from such events is an important way of keeping the mission and its desired outcomes in front of the church as well as promoting wider acceptance and adoption of the mission, vision, values, and strategy throughout the church.

By continuously promoting the celebration of wins and visible milestones within the context of the church's culture, strategy, mission, and values, the overseer is both leading change in the culture and keeping at the front of members' awareness the "what" of the mission and the "how" of the strategy for mission fulfillment.

Making Hard Decisions

Overseers must accept the responsibility for making clear-eyed assessments of the church's strengths and weaknesses, and then they must follow through in making the difficult choices required to bring about improvement. As they review components like staff, programming, organization, structure, leadership, planning, systems, and pace of ministry, they need to be able to accurately evaluate areas of relative weakness and strength.

(Image 18)

THE TOOLKIT | Making Hard Decisions

Rate the following areas of your church's ministry as it exists today:

	WEAKNESS	MODERATE WEAKNESS	NEUTRAL	MODERATE STRENGTH	STRENGTH
Staff					
Programming					
Organization					
Structure					
Leadership					
Planning					
Systems					
Pace					

That done, the overseer should prioritize the areas where improvement is needed, from greatest need to least need, and should then prayerfully consider the following questions:

◇   What needs to be done to address our greatest weakness?

◇   Who has to understand this need along with me?

◇ How will I go about helping them see and understand the issue?

◇ What process do we need to follow to execute this decision or improvement? (with steps listed in order)

Even with difficult decisions, breaking the process down into steps of assessment, recruitment of needed assistance, and mapping out procedure can help the overseer approach the situation with greater calm and deliberation and correspondingly greater chances of success. And of course, as in all matters concerning church revitalization, the overseer should be ever conscious of working alongside Jesus to form the church into what it needs to be to fulfill the Great Commission in its community. You do not face these decisions alone; God is working through you to help His people fulfill His vision.

Carl Willis wouldn't look at either Pastor Bob or Lance, the youth minister, as he sat down. Bob gave Lance a quick glance and received a small shrug in reply.

"Carl, thanks for meeting with Pastor Lance and me today. I appreciate—"

"We can skip the formalities, Pastor," Carl said, cutting Bob off. "I know why I've been called in here, so we might as well get to it."

Bob paused long enough to take a couple of deep breaths. "Carl, would it be all right if we started with a prayer?"

He shrugged; his eyes were still firmly fixed on the tabletop in front of him.

Bob led a brief prayer, asking God to attend to what was about to be said and to increase in each of the three of them a sense of his grace and love. When he finished, he studied Carl for a few seconds.

"Carl, Pastor Lance tells me you've expressed some objections to the direction of our high school ministry."

"I don't have a problem with the ministry," Carl snapped. "I have a problem with some of the kids in the ministry."

"How is that different, Carl?" Lance asked. "Andrea and the other kids in her class are doing some amazing things. Their faith is growing. They're serving this community in ways our youth group has never done before. They're bringing in kids who've never heard the gospel and—"

"I don't want my daughter around some of those kids," Carl said. He was looking at both of them now, his eyes wide with emotion. "I don't trust them, even when they're in a Sunday School classroom. And I sure don't like my daughter and her friends going over to those apartments on Robinson Street, knocking on doors where who-knows-what has been going on."

"Carl, have you talked to Andrea about any of this?" Bob said quietly. "What is she telling you? Has anything happened to her that we need to know about?"

Carl crossed his arms in front of him and said nothing.

"We're serious about bringing people to Jesus, Carl," Bob said. "We want the people on Robinson Street to know him, just as much as we want Andrea and the other kids who've grown up at Grace Community to know him. The outreach that Pastor Lance has organized is a key part of that goal. You need to understand that."

Carl shook his head. "Why can't we have a separate class for those kids, where they can learn what they need to know without—"

"Without a chance to talk to committed Christian kids like Andrea?" Bob said. "Without being able to feel that they are loved and cared for in this church, just as much as we love and care for you and your family? Carl, what you're talking about is not in line with our calling here at Grace Community Church."

"Then maybe I need to leave," Carl muttered.

"You could do that," Lance said, "but it would be a shame. Andrea is really plugged in to the high school group. I think it might be a tough thing for her, adjusting to some other church."

"Well, I can see where this is headed," Carl said, getting out of his chair. "I don't think I have anything else to say."

"I do, Carl," Bob said in a firm voice. "As your pastor, who is responsible to God for your soul, I need you to know that you are dangerously close to putting yourself on a path of disobedience and endangering your daughter's faith at the same time. You need to spend some time in careful reflection and prayer before you make a decision that you're likely to regret."

Carl stared at them both for a few seconds, then walked out.

Lance took a deep breath and puffed out his cheeks as he let it out. "Well... that could've gone better."

Bob Dunbar shook his head. "Carl needs our prayers and our compassion," he said. "Along with Andrea." He looked carefully at Lance. "But we cannot permit an attitude like that to derail the Kingdom progress we're making. And before God, we will not."

Leading Change

In his book *Leading Change*, author John Kotter makes the point that for any organization to implement successful, long-term change, it must have leaders who can articulate a vision, inspire and empower others to embrace the vision, and equip others in the organization to implement the vision at a tactical, hands-on level.[1]

I hope that by now, these principles sound very familiar! The fact is that as an over-seer leading a church through the revitalization process, you must incorporate these same competencies, in the context of your mission, values, and strategy, in order to guide your church toward fulfilling the Great Commission.

The good news here is that you have tools at your disposal to help you execute each of these competencies. And, as with the tools we've already discussed, they are almost infinitely customizable, depending on the specific needs of your church's cultural and community setting.

Preach Your Way through Problems

Have you ever wondered why the American presidency is sometimes referred to as a "bully pulpit"? The term was coined by President Theodore Roosevelt (1901–09), and what he meant was that as president, he had the frequent opportunity to use the prominence of his office to advocate for his desired agenda. He found the presidential platform (his "pulpit") to be superb ("bully") for these purposes.

Overseers—most of whom are preaching pastors—have a similar tool at their disposal for leading change in their churches. By prayerfully designing your preaching schedule around the central issues facing your church as you carry out your God-given mission, you will be able to communicate clearly to members about the spiritual needs of the congregation and also about how their individual growth in faith and discipleship can impact those needs.

Your preaching plan should take into account significant events in the life of the church and its members, as well as important matters and developments in the surrounding community. It will be especially important to consider the implications of upcoming mile-stones in the annual plan, considering their implications for the spiritual development of members and its place in the ongoing disciple-making strategy of the church.

Meaningful Meetings

In the business world, many regard meetings as obstructions to getting actual work done. But as the overseer of a church in the revitalization process, you can use well-planned and strategically considered meetings as a principal tool for effectively leading change.

From the "Leadership Summit," where staff and other leaders receive the commu-nication of the vision and are trained in what they need to know to carry it forward; to monthly or weekly meetings with staff, team leaders, or other significant groups to assess progress and address challenges; effective meetings can be vital to an overseer's ability to announce, explain, and guide the process of cultural change in the church.

The key, of course, is to maintain the vision, mission, strategy, and values as top-of-mind elements in every setting. Doing this will also bring a focus to meetings that keeps everyone aligned with how the matters at hand impact the overarching aims of the mission.

Vision-Driven Planning

As you read and consider the various planning elements in this book, you should notice that every question, every tactical decision, and every element of planning proceeds out of its contribution to the achievement of your church's vision. This is why our vision expression takes the shape of a pyramid. When developing the mission, values, and strategy, overseers are asked to consider them in the context of the vision God has placed before the church. When considering the key leaders who will be needed to implement the revitalization process, the overseer should choose those with the attributes most necessary to the vision. At every stage, the overseer should be asking, "How does this plan/change/group leader/sermon/evangelism effort/mission statement/goal get us closer to achieving the Great Commission for this church?" In other words, everything about the church revitalization process, from the initial selection of those on the leadership team to the timing and nature of the events celebrating completion, should be geared toward and contribute to the achievement of the mission.

This holds true for the overseer's planning around communicating the *ReFocus* plan to leaders and members, for evaluating plan progress, and for establishing the components of each annual plan in the multi-year cycle. Vision drives your prayer life concerning the revitalization effort. It guides how you craft your mission statement, both verbally and visually. It determines what you preach about and when you preach it.

As an overseer, you can never over-emphasize the importance of vision and revelation to the spiritual health of the church (Proverbs 29:18). God's empowering vision must be at the forefront of all you do. We refer to this as vision saturation. As you select the tools you need for the journey, let vision-driven planning guide each choice you make.

Benefits of the Right Tools

By now, I hope you've come to appreciate that, though the church revitalization process requires exacting thought, prayerful planning, and constant attention to detail, it also comes with the resources and help you need to execute efficiently and lead for revitalization. Whether you are dealing with difficult individuals who are resistant to change, counseling team leaders and groups to encourage them in their discipleship, or proclaiming the vision from the pulpit, your work as overseer will be facilitated by making use of the tools you have chosen and designed for the needs of your church and its community setting.

The Right Tools Help You Persevere

So much of maintaining the integrity of the process, as well as your own commitment to it, is predicated on making the right decisions at the right times. The tools we've discussed in this chapter will help you do that, by breaking down each inflection point to simple, manageable steps that you can work through with your leadership team.

These tools, along with many others found in the *ReFocus* notebook, can provide you with the granular knowledge you need to guide your church toward fulfilling its mission. They can also be a source of confidence, as you step out in faith, that you are doing the right things in the right way, and in the right order. The work of an overseer can be lonely, but knowing that you have the resources you need to fulfill your calling can help you stay strong in your leadership walk.

The Right Tools Help You Chart Your Progress

Staying on course during the revitalization process requires constant measurement as the overseer and other leaders analyze outcomes, compare them with identified benchmarks, and evaluate the church's progress toward completing its annual plans. By utilizing the tools available, overseers are better able to assess how individual members are progressing in their discipleship journey and how that progress is impacting the church's advancement toward the fulfillment of the mission.

The Right Tools Help You Celebrate

As the church moves steadily along the way toward revitalization, you also have the tools you need to decide when and how to celebrate the important victories and milestones. By knowing what is most important to your church and the values that inform its mission, you will be able to formulate the commemoration of the church's "wins" in the way that connects most effectively with the minds and hearts of both the leaders and the general membership of your church.

———————

By identifying and using the proper tools, overseers can effectively lead change and partner with God in transforming the culture of the church. The ultimate goal, of course, is to bring about a broad-based commitment to disciple-making in the membership: both internally, as each member grows in faith and understanding; and externally, as each disciple goes out and tells those outside the church, "Come and see." In this, we follow Christ, our great exemplar, who has provided the empowering vision and clearly stated the mission.

Overseers who use these tools wisely and well can be assured that they are participating with God in building His masterpiece, His "workmanship, created in Christ Jesus for good works" (Ephesians 2:10). Empowered by the Spirit and guided by the word of the Lord, they are faithful workers building a house for the Lord, and they do not labor in vain (Psalm 127:1).

———————

Notes

1. John Kotter, *Leading Change* (Boston: Harvard Business Review Press, 2012)

PART
4

Get on with
God's Plan

11

Balancing the Three Essential Leadership Roles

James Thomas could see the tears glistening in Esther Callan's eyes. He scooted the box of tissues closer to her side of the small table. She pulled a tissue and daubed at her eyes.

"Thank you, Pastor. I thought I'd be able to get through this conversation without getting emotional."

"It's okay, Esther. It's a sad thing when people leave the church; emotions are certainly permissible."

She looked at him and shook her head slowly. "I just can't understand what those young families are thinking. Sanford Memorial is growing like never before; we're reaching new people every day. I can feel a sense of purpose here that has been missing for so long. What reason could they possibly have for walking away from that?"

Jim took a deep breath and settled deeper into his chair. "Esther, before I say anything else, I want you to hear and believe me when I tell you that we did everything we could to keep them here at Sanford Memorial Church. The church leadership and I prayed over this for hours; I met with each of the families on multiple occasions to hear their concerns and try to explain why the church needs to maintain the course we're on. And in the end, it just wasn't enough."

"They wouldn't listen?"

Pastor Jim shook his head slowly. "They demanded things that would have completely sabotaged our God-given mission, Esther. In the end, they made their ongoing participation and financial stewardship conditional on some things that were not in our future. We had no choice but to part ways." Jim sighed. "And in reality, they already had one foot out the door, anyway."

Esther stared into an empty corner of the office. "That must have been so difficult."

"Probably among the most uncomfortable and painful conversations I've ever had as a pastor," Jim said, nodding. "And make no mistake—these were families who were financially capable of making a big difference in the church budget."

"But you can't serve two masters," Esther said softly.

"I couldn't have said it better myself," Jim said with a sad smile.

Children have many endearing qualities, and one of my favorites is their transparency and guilelessness. With a child, you rarely have to wonder what they're thinking; it usually spills out into the open, either with their words or their behavior.

I remember playing "hide and seek" with my own children as toddlers, and I still smile when I think about their technique for "hiding": putting their hands over their eyes. Their mental process is on full display: *If I can't see you, then I must be invisible!* There is nothing more sweetly amusing than seeing a little one standing in the middle of the room with their hands over their eyes, confident that they are hidden from the onlookers they can't see.

Unfortunately, this is a case of "childhood logic" that doesn't age well. Far too many adults who should know better still believe that if they can't see a problem, it doesn't exist. And we know all too well the likely outcome of that attitude, especially when it's exhibited by leaders.

The business landscape is littered with examples. Beginning with its founding in 1892 and for nearly a hundred years, Sears (originally Sears and Roebuck) was the dominant retailer in America. The "Sears catalog" held a place of honor in most households second only to the family Bible; many a childhood wish sprang into being after a viewing of the Christmas edition. But the leaders of the company failed to anticipate or see the threat to the Sears business model that was posed by, first, big-box discounters like Walmart, and later, online retail behemoth Amazon. The once-mighty Sears retail empire filed for bankruptcy protection in 2018. Similarly, Nokia, the Finnish tech firm that by 1998 was the world's dominant manufacturer of mobile phones, failed to understand the implications of Apple's development of the iPhone. As a result, the company lost most of its market share by 2010, ultimately surviving only because of its purchase by Microsoft Corporation.

Tragically, the same thing happens to churches. As we stated in the introduction of this book, as of the book's publication, as many as 90 percent of the churches in the West are in some stage of decline. In the vast majority of cases, this is because the leaders of the churches have failed to exercise proper "oversight" in the classic sense: they have not raised their eyes sufficiently from the present to anticipate how their churches need to be positioned for the future.

You *Are* an Overseer, but Are You a Skilled One?

Apart from God's word and the Holy Spirit, the greatest single influence on a church is its pastor. As a pastor, your character, competence, teaching, and day-to-day interaction with members and staff will, in addition to your theology and ministry priorities, shape the church and inform its direction more than any other factor.

As a pastor, you are charged with leading God's people to a growing faith and more committed discipleship. This necessitates that you should be looking ahead, anticipating, and constantly asking yourself questions like, "What is God's vision for this church and its impact on this community and the world?"; "How is the community changing, and how does the church need to change in order to better fulfill the Great Commission in this time and place?"; "Are our members becoming more dedicated, committed disciples of Jesus? And are they making new disciples?" Your answers to these questions must then propel you toward pursuing these godly aims in your church, leading the changes necessary to ensure that the church is on a continual journey of revitalization, rather than receding toward decline.

Envisioning and Implementing

To successfully ask and answer questions like these, the skilled overseer must be competent at both *envisioning* what needs to happen and *implementing* a plan for bringing about the desired result. But the problem revealed by research is that only ten percent of pastors are innately good at both. In fact, many of us fall more readily into one category or the other: "idea" people who can readily see the grand design but may have challenges with purposeful pursuit of the steps required for its fulfillment; or "worker bees" who are prone to adhere faithfully to the task and attend to each detail, but who may sometimes lose focus on the ultimate purpose and destination.

But the better news is that the 90 percent who are less inclined toward one end or another of this continuum can, with good coaching and hard work, learn the skills needed to fill in their deficiencies. In fact, a chief purpose of the *ReFocus* process for church revitalization is to help pastors become well-equipped with the practical skills and habits of mind that will empower them to cast a powerful vision *and* lead the church through the process of its realization.

Balancing the Three Essential Leadership Roles

In Acts 20:17–38, we read of the tender, tearful parting words between Paul and the elders of his beloved church at Ephesus, a place where, as Paul himself says, he lived and "taught you publicly from house to house," declaring "to both Jews and Greeks that they must turn to God in repentance and have faith in our Lord Jesus." Paul closes his speech with these words of admonition, directed specifically at the elders of the Ephesian church:

> *Be on guard for yourselves and for all the flock, among which the Holy Spirit has made you overseers, to shepherd the church of God, which He purchased with His own blood (Acts 20:28).*

Peter shares similar admonition in his first letter. Look again at his words:

> *Therefore, I exhort the elders among you, as your fellow elder and*
> *witness of the sufferings of Christ, and a partaker also of the glory*
> *that is to be revealed, shepherd the flock of God among you, exer-*
> *cising oversight not under compulsion, but voluntarily, according*
> *to the will of God; and nor for sordid gain, but with eagerness; nor*
> *yet as lording it over those allotted to your charge, but proving to*
> *be examples to the flock. And when the Chief Shepherd appears,*
> *you will receive the unfading crown of glory (1 Peter 5:1–4).*

Clearly, the biblical role for leaders, as envisioned by Paul and Peter, comprises the three roles of elder, shepherd, and overseer. Pastors who are leading a church through the revitalization process must be attentive to honing their skillsets along the lines of these three particular biblical roles. They must function as 1) a wise elder; 2) a skilled overseer; and 3) a transformational shepherd. Notice, too, that the three roles each have a preceding descriptor. These descriptors are specific to the work of church revitalization. Wisdom, skill, and transformation are essential to the work of revitalization.

All three are essential, but the problem is that most of the time, the particular behaviors and attitudes required by the three roles are imbalanced. As alluded to early in the book, most pastors enter the work with more-than-adequate skills as shepherds (providing pastoral care and concern for their churches) and elders (knowledgeable about spiritual matters and able to teach effectively), but woefully underprepared as overseers (possessing strategic vision and the ability to effect needed change). The tendency I have observed in my years of work with churches, in fact, is that instead of being equally balanced among the three roles, most pastors spend about 60 percent of their time as shepherds, 30 percent as elders, and only about 10 percent as overseers.

The training provided by the Church *ReFocus* process is aimed at redressing this imbalance. By providing biblical guidance and means for detailed and accurate self-assessment, the goal is to help pastors understand where their skills and understandings require reinforcement to produce balanced leadership. I am not advocating that all a pastor needs to do is the work of an overseer. What I am advocating for is the necessity of finding the rightful place for the work of the overseer within the overall work of the pastor.

CHAPTER 11

The Wise Elder

As pastors prepare themselves to lead the church in revitalization, three qualities are essential for them to fulfill the role of wise elder. They must:

1. Demonstrate wisdom in seeking God and leading his people;

2. Demonstrate character that builds trust;

3. Communicate with inspiration.

Toward these ends, pastors wishing to assess their readiness for this role should be asking themselves questions like these:

⬦ Am I well-rounded and spiritually mature?

⬦ Is my identity founded in Christ, rather than what others say about me?

⬦ Am I able to listen to and understand what others are saying?

⬦ Am I able to discern God's will and direction?

⬦ Do my words and deeds reflect the nature of Christ?

⬦ Can I be looked to as a model for good attitudes and right behavior?

⬦ Do others consider me a trusted counselor?

⬦ Does my preaching challenge the status quo?

⬦ Can I talk about difficult topics in a way that invites further inquiry?

⬦ Does my teaching express genuine, heartfelt beliefs?

By considering these and many other similar questions, pastors may be able to evaluate their readiness to accept and carry out the leadership responsibilities of the wise elder.

The Skilled Overseer

Typically the least evident of the three leadership functions, the skilled overseer is nevertheless a role that can be learned and practiced effectively. The skilled overseer must:

1. Know how to lead a change process in the church;

2. Be able to cast vision boldly and implement strategy effectively;

3. Be able to align resources and execute daily tasks.

Preparing for these capabilities will require the overseer to seek the answers to questions such as:

◊ Do I see where the church needs to go, and am I willing to take steps in that direction?

◊ Have I accurately assessed the current realities of the church?

◊ Do I routinely seek out challenges and opportunities for the church?

◊ Do I have a clearly articulated plan to help the church take its next step?

◊ Do others believe me to be a strategic thinker?

◊ Am I able to assign tasks and hold others accountable for ministry?

◊ Can I support and encourage others to carry out ministry?

◊ Am I able to secure the resources necessary for accomplishing ministry?

To develop the skills and mindsets of the skilled overseer, which are so central to leading a church through the revitalization process, pastors should spend prayerful time in deep consideration of these questions and consider grappling with the biblical typology of the overseer (as presented in chapter 1) in an in-depth personal study. You will need to be self-aware to identify weaknesses and have a plan to develop the necessary strengths in areas where you currently struggle. The knowledge you will acquire as a result will be invaluable.

The Transformational Shepherd

Though many pastors are already skilled in their shepherding role by inclination and intention, there are still next steps that should be taken in order to become the truly transformational shepherds needed to lead church revitalization. The transformational shepherd should be able to:

1. Love and care for people as transformation occurs;

2. Gather and influence people in the cause of personal and church transformation;

3. Respectfully correct misplaced values.

When evaluating readiness for carrying out the role of transformational shepherd, pastors will do well to consider questions such as:

◊ Am I more interested in giving to and equipping others or getting what I need from them?

◊ Am I able to perceive when someone is struggling spiritually?

◊ Do I feel the desire to help those who are struggling?

◊ Do I typically praise people for a job well done?

◊ Do I seek out opportunities to spend time with people?

◊ Do others look to me for wisdom and guidance?

◊ Am I able to easily engage others in conversation?

◊ Can I accurately assess others' strengths and weaknesses?

◊ Do I have the ability to speak truthfully and forthrightly without putting others off unnecessarily?

◊ Am I generally forgiving, even in the face of offensive behavior?

◊ Do I possess enough self-confidence to not always require others' approval?

When pastors have given due consideration and honestly considered these and other questions, they are prepared to more accurately assess their readiness to become transformational shepherds for the church.

Take a moment to contemplate the descriptive words attached to the three central roles for pastors leading church transformation:

◊ Elders should be *wise*;

◊ Overseers should be *skilled*;

◊ Shepherds should be *transformational.*

These descriptors have been chosen with great care and abundant research because they are essential for preparing pastors to effectively lead churches through the revitalization process. In their role as elders, pastors must exhibit wisdom because, among other reasons, persons lacking in wisdom are usually also lacking the foresight that all good leaders must possess. As skilled overseers, pastors must be able not only to anticipate challenges and opportunities facing the church but also be able to lead the change and adaptation necessary to meet them. Transformational shepherds excel at comforting and mentoring those in their care, but they are also intentional about not leaving them where they are. Rather, they encourage and lead them on toward greater spiritual maturity.

Your Most Powerful Tool Is Vision

As we have already noted, in churches—as in almost any collection of people who are gathered for some purpose—nothing is more powerful than culture. For that reason, pastors must possess the most detailed knowledge possible of their churches' existing culture. Unless the pastor knows where the church is, they cannot possibly lead the church to where it needs to be.

The place where pastors must start to change the culture is by effectively casting a vision of God's desired outcome for the church. And to do that, pastors must understand and be prepared for how receptive the church will be to the vision. Remember: "A vision without a task is but a dream; a task without a vision is drudgery; but a vision and task are the hope of the world."

Churches with a high degree of vision receptivity will be easier to inspire and move toward the necessary change to make the vision a reality. Churches with lower vision receptivity will require more careful thought, preparation, and planning to move them successfully along the path toward revitalization. The pastor will also need to devote more time to developing necessary skillsets and competencies.

In assessing vision receptivity, pastors will need to consider questions around shared understandings of purpose among staff and members, enthusiasm for ministry both inside and outside the church, expectations about how resources are used, degree of prayerfulness, trust among members and in leadership, willingness to attempt new things, communication throughout the church, engagement, and other vital matters.

Your Most Difficult Challenge Is Culture

It's important to remember that the reason churches enter decline is almost certainly because their culture has drifted away from a focus on making and sending disciples of Jesus. This means that the number-one task for pastors leading churches toward revitalization is leading change in the culture.

Cultural change doesn't happen overnight and almost certainly will involve some degree of conflict. After all, people living in a world going through change at the blinding speed we observe all around us often seek out church as a place of comfort and reassurance; for many, this means that they want things to feel familiar. They may even wish for church to be like it was when they were younger, which is almost certainly going to conflict with the church's need to remain engaged with current culture—to be "in the world" while not being "of the world."

Pastors leading cultural change, therefore, need high competency in managing and resolving conflict in spiritually informed ways, keeping in mind these principles:

◇ Conflict is inevitable.

◇ Conflict should be addressed promptly.

◇ Healthy, managed conflict is necessary for change to occur.

◇ If conflict is not managed in healthy ways, it will become destructive.

◇ The way a pastor leads through conflict largely determines whether the conflict will be constructive or destructive.

◇ God is not the author of chaos; rather, God provides qualities that lead to peace.

◇ Prior unresolved conflict in churches often becomes embedded in the culture and contributes to ongoing conflict during change processes.

◇ As people mature spiritually and emotionally, they become less likely to initiate destructive conflict.

Factors within the church such as stress, power struggles, the presence or rate of change, unmet needs, conflicting views of reality, and others are typical sources and drivers of conflict. It's easy to see that when churches are going through a process of revitalization, many of these factors will be in play as the culture shifts from the status quo to what it needs to be in order for God's mission to be achieved.

What the competent pastor must always keep in mind is that some issues are so foundational that conflict around them must not be avoided, but rather managed in a spirit of love, respect, and spiritual maturity. When conflict arises concerning biblical truth, biblical morality, the mission of the church, church unity, or concerning character, integrity, and truth, avoidance or compromise for the sake of "maintaining the peace" can be fatal to not only the revitalization process but also the very life and integrity of the church.

Resilience Is the Key

In his book *Leadership Jazz: The Essential Elements of a Great Leader,* Max De Pree views leadership as more like leading a jazz combo than conducting a symphony orchestra. Though both groups—and their leaders—are concerned with making beautiful, coherent music, jazz ensembles feature improvisation by individual performers, with the "lead" circulating among various members of the group as the rest of the performers remain attuned to the tempo, the energy level, and the ever-changing "feel" of the music.[1]

Similarly, leading a church through the revitalization process involves constant attention to evolving situations, careful and ongoing assessment of progress, and support of the various "players" as they, in turn, support the components of the strategy and mission. To put it simply, it's a lot! Such a task requires energy, focus, dedication, and hours spent in prayer and spiritual discernment. It's no wonder, then, that one of the major obstacles faced by overseers is burnout. Burnout can originate from a moral failure, exposure to incessant conflict, escapist behavior, discouragement, or simple fatigue.

The solution to burnout for overseers seeking to lead a church toward revitalization is resilience. Merriam-Webster defines resilience as "an ability to recover from or adjust easily to misfortune or change." In physics terms, resiliency denotes the ability of an object to absorb energy from an impact and quickly return to its former shape. Both definitions capture accurately a quality essential to the overseer: the ability to "spring back" from difficulty or trauma and re-engage productively with the tasks of spiritual leadership.

The nine Fruits of the Spirit (Galatians 5:22–23) may be subdivided into sets of three attributes that align with the three principal components of resiliency as required of overseers leading a church toward revitalization. *Love, joy,* and *peace* may be understood as indicating the overseer's spiritual vitality, born of a deep relationship with God. *Patience, kindness,* and *goodness* are indicative of how we function in relationship to others. *Faithfulness, gentleness,* and *self-control* indicate our personal stability amid changing circumstances.

1. **SPIRITUAL VITALITY *(love, joy, peace)*—**produced through a deep and abiding relationship with God. As Jesus describes in John 15:5: "Whoever abides in me and I in him, he it is that bears much fruit, for apart from me you can do nothing." This sense of rootedness, of "abiding" in Christ, anchors the overseer as God's child: one who bears the fruits of love, joy, and peace that demonstrate and validate that rootedness.

2. **RELATIONAL TENACITY *(patience, kindness, goodness)*—**the ability to have and maintain relationships with others that are simultaneously hopeful and realistic. Overseers must possess the ability to stay in relationships even when they are challenging as people deal with the struggles that inevitably come from seeking deeper relationship with Jesus and others. In this context the spiritual fruits of patience, kindness, and goodness in the overseer's life cause him to be an inviting presence for those who need to work through conflict, offer and receive forgiveness, and work proactively to accomplish ministry.

3. **PERSONAL STABILITY *(faithfulness, gentleness, self-control)*—**the capacity to remain balanced and self-possessed while pursuing Christ's mission and fulfilling the calling of the overseer. Spiritual leaders who act impulsively, inconsistently, or selfishly portray the opposite of this quality. But those who exhibit stability—even in the midst of the sometimes-chaotic process of leading change—demonstrate the spiritual fruits of faithfulness, gentleness, and self-control that are so vital to the overseer's ministry to the church.

By measuring themselves against these qualities and the fruits of the Spirit that they demonstrate, overseers may assess their degree of resilience (*Image 19*) and also work to strengthen any deficiencies that might present obstacles to their leadership of the revitalization process.

Image 19

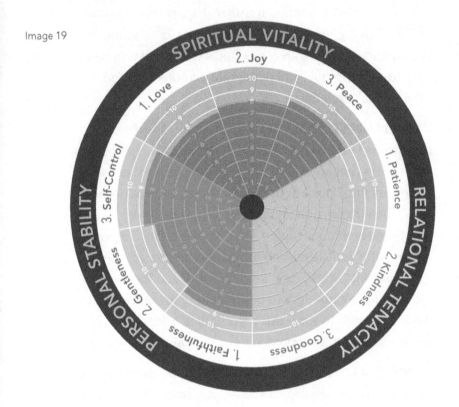

Dreaming God's Dream for Your Church

Overseers who have captured God's vision for their churches and who have accepted the spiritual responsibility for leading the church toward fulfillment of the vision face a passage that is perhaps the most challenging and rewarding journey for any follower of Christ. It is a journey full of both deep joys and heartbreaking disappointments. But it is also a path that must be walked in the full recognition of the spiritual equipping that God provides through faith.

For this reason, the ministry of revitalization must flow from a life filled with the fruits of the Spirit and firmly rooted in the skills of the overseer. This orientation allows an overseer to remain fresh, engaged, and passionate. Certainly, there will be seasons when dogged, faithful determination will be necessary, but faithfulness and tenacity are not qualities that should exclude the joy, peace, and love overflowing from a heart dedicated to seeing the Great Commission carried out in the church.

Overseers whose hearts are empowered by and overflowing with the fruits of the Spirit are able to envision the dreams of God for the church and then faithfully lead the church toward making those dreams a reality. 2 Peter 1:3 tells us, "His divine power has granted to us all things that pertain to life and godliness, through the knowledge of Him who called us to His own glory and excellence." Never forget that God empowers those whom He calls; as you dream His dream for your church, He is within you, ready to provide, strengthen, and inspire.

———————————

Notes

1. Max DePree, *Leadership Jazz: The Essential Elements of a Great Leader*, Revised Edition (Sydney, Australia, 2008)

CHAPTER
12

The Bright Future for Overseers

In 2014, the World Economic Forum (WEF) commissioned an important study. The WEF is an international non-governmental organization founded in 1971 to study issues affecting global communities and to lobby international lawmakers for positive change. The study, published in 2015, was entitled "Outlook on the Global Agenda," and it contains a survey of experts and thought leaders from around the world with the intent of surfacing the most pressing issues facing the world today.[1]

An overwhelming 86% of respondents believed that the international community was suffering from a crisis in leadership. In the wake of a global financial crisis and in contemplation of difficulties related to the climate, widespread poverty, terrorism, and other ongoing calamities, those surveyed identified this vulnerability for international leaders as a paramount challenge to be solved.

As we look at how things have developed since 2015, most of us would probably agree that the international climate for leadership has not improved much. In the intervening years, we've experienced ongoing violence throughout the world, a global pandemic, and the outbreak of wars that have led to a discussion about the use of nuclear weapons. In other words, our world's need for leaders who can step up and move society in positive directions has only grown more urgent—and their absence more obvious.

What Does the Future Require?

But perhaps there is a bit of good news amid this grim landscape. Christians know that the love of Christ is the only permanent cure for the ills that plague humankind. As the church embraces the Lord's Great Commission and advances the kingdom of the Prince of Peace, God's will for humanity will unfold in grace and blessing for the entire world. The words of the beloved song describe it well: "... in His name all oppression shall cease."

To carry out this God-given mission, though, the church will require visionary overseers who can lead God's people toward the realization of God's transforming vision. As Mordecai said of his cousin Esther, overseers are being called forward "for just such a time as this" to lead the change needed in local churches: transformational change that will re-fashion them as outposts of the Kingdom—places where disciples are being formed, matured, and sent out to plant the Gospel message in other human hearts.

The Church Needs Revitalization

Make no mistake: the need for revitalization in the church has never been greater. With some 90% of Western churches in decline, the time has passed for another church growth strategy, another sermon series on discipleship, another outreach campaign, another leadership conference. As valuable and well-intentioned as these efforts may be, they are not enough. To meet the needs of a rapidly changing world, the church must be revitalized and its leaders must be taught, equipped, and deployed. The church must be fundamentally refocused on its central mission as defined by Christ: making and sending out transformed and committed disciples of Jesus.

For revitalization to occur, churches on the "back side of the curve" must face the inadequacies of their ingrained ways of thinking and existing strategies that have brought them to the present situation. Revitalizing churches will need to grapple with uncomfortable, yet necessary questions like "Why do we exist?" "What should we preserve?" "What must we stop doing?" Churches will be ineffective at advancing the Kingdom in today's world until they accept the reality that they must change their understandings of the organization, its mission, and the needs of the surrounding community.

The Overseer Must Lead Revitalization

But churches cannot engage constructively with these profound questions without the leadership of visionary overseers who have the understanding, the training, and perhaps most important, the resilience to develop the path forward and then guide their churches along that path. As Paul said in Romans 10:14, how will they hear, without someone to tell them?

It's also important to keep in mind that the overseer must be more than a skilled motivator or a charismatic speaker. While these abilities are certainly valuable, they must be placed alongside the ability to assess, to position their churches properly in the local community, to cast vision, to set goals, to make disciples, and to develop leaders. They must be able to clearly perceive strengths and weaknesses in the local body of believers; they must have the knowledge to create plans designed around the specific needs and resources of the church and the community; they require wisdom and patience to guide others in the implementation of those plans.

Indeed, the role of the overseer in leading revitalization requires a tremendous amount of mental, emotional, and spiritual energy from the pastor who is guiding the effort called for in the *ReFocus* process. Some may look at all this and think, "Who has time to do all that?" After all, pastors are very busy people, even if all they do is keep up with staff meetings, funerals, births, illnesses, weddings, social events, community involvement—not to mention sermon preparation!

And yet, the alternative is not acceptable. Failing to take up the challenge and embrace the opportunity for church revitalization is to consign the church to a position of ever-decreasing relevance and dwindling impact in society.

This is why the process, methods, and strategies we have outlined here are so vital. Through the *ReFocus* process, pastors can find the tools they need, make essential discoveries about their churches, and develop the vision toward which the Holy Spirit is calling each church as it embraces its role in fulfilling the Great Commission in its community. Once you have learned the skillsets involved in being an overseer, you will wonder how you ever pastored without them.

Pastor Bob Dunbar felt tears tickling the corners of his eyes, then spilling out onto his cheeks. He didn't bother to wipe them away; this moment was too enormous and beautiful to worry about how his emotions might appear to someone else.

The sanctuary of Grace Community Church was packed; it held just over 3,500 people at full capacity, and Bob couldn't see a single empty seat. The positive energy and love radiating from the congregation were palpable.

Seated in the front rows nearest the podium were the young people who were about to be commissioned as leaders in the Power

Pods, the fellowship and accountability groups that had formed throughout the Robinson Street community as a result of the outreach program developed and implemented by Pastor Lance and the other leaders in the youth ministry. In a few moments, Bob would invite them to join him on the platform, where they would be surrounded by their small-group leaders, the elders and deacons of the church, and the ministry staff. They would appoint the kids as leaders in their groups: responsible to pray for, advise, guide, and serve their peers as they all tried to become more like Jesus. Bob would pray over them as the leaders in the church placed their hands on them, sending them out to serve their neighborhood and each other in the name of Jesus.

As Bob listened to the worship team leading the church in the final chorus before he would go to the podium, he studied the faces of the soon-to-be-commissioned leaders. Few of these high-school-age kids had been raised in a church-going environment; several of them had seen more trouble in their young lives than many much older people. But due to the Power Pod ministry envisioned by Pastor Lance as part of the church's annual ministry plan for this fifth year of the revitalization process, these young men and women were getting to know Jesus, being served and offering service in his name, and becoming salt and light in their community. Lance had told Bob recently that there were easily as many kids in Power Pod group meetings in the Robinson Street neighborhood each week as were coming to the Grace Community campus for more traditional Bible study times. Young people were coming to Jesus, the youth ministry was baptizing more new Christians than ever, and lives were being shaped for service.

The song was over. Bob motioned for the people to be seated as he approached the podium, trying to swallow around the lump in his throat. *Thank you, Lord,* he prayed silently. *Thank you for bringing us to this day.*

CHAPTER 12

The Perpetual Need for Revitalization

If you have read this far, I hope that your spiritual imagination has been kindled and that the Holy Spirit has placed in your heart a vision for what your church could become as a result of following the *ReFocus* process. I hope that you are envisioning a time of great fruitfulness in ministry: a day when you and everyone in your church can take deep satisfaction from the bountiful harvest that God has supplied as a result of the church answering the call to revitalization.

But what overseers must keep in mind is that when that day comes—as glorious and fulfilling as it will be—the story will not end. The need for church revitalization and refocus on the Great Commission will continue. Even as they rejoice in the successes secured for the Kingdom, churches must be in the continual posture of reaching forward, aiming for fulfillment of the next empowering vision. Overseers must always be raising their vision to the next horizon, leading the church toward the next goal, the next mission, the next Kingdom-building opportunity that God is placing on their hearts. In other words, until Christ returns, the church will persist in a constant state of need for revitalization. We must never be content to hold the territory we already possess: the Great Commission calls us ever forward until there is no person on earth who has not been granted the opportunity to follow after Jesus and no Christian who is not being shaped daily into His likeness.

Every Pastor an Overseer

At the most basic level, the role of overseer involves skills in stewardship, leadership, organization, administration, and other abilities that many pastors may not innately possess—and which, unfortunately, they may have had few opportunities to learn during their time in seminary or other traditional pastoral training settings. But the better news is that, by following the principles in this book and taking advantage of available mentorship opportunities, these skills can be learned—and you can learn them!

In fact, if the church is to effectively carry out its God-given mission in the world, it will be vital for every pastor to become equipped as an overseer: ready to lead change and capable of envisioning, shaping, and implementing a plan for effecting change in the local church. The goal of the *ReFocus* process is, first, to empower and equip pastors to become "champions" for their churches by acquiring and honing their skills as vision casters, administrators and organizers, strategists, culture creators and nurturers, and developers of other leaders and members. Then, we help pastors gain the insights and tools they need to lead their churches in the specific directions required by their unique setting in the community and the vision God has placed on the pastor's heart.

The *ReFocus* process is predicated on the belief that every pastor can become a competent and confident overseer for the church. By learning and executing the skills of adaptive leadership, overseers can provide the visionary guidance each church needs to fulfill its God-given mission. Certainly, every pastor is different, just as every church is different. No two paths to revitalization will look exactly the same. But the strength of the *ReFocus* process is that it is designed to draw out of pastors their individual qualities, then channel and augment them in a way that enhances the pastor's ability to serve as a steward, advocate, and trusted leader who can help the church become all that God intends.

———

Ken Perry had barely seated himself behind his desk when a knock came on his office door. He walked over and opened it to see his father standing in the church hallway.

"I thought you might be here," his dad said. "I was hoping to catch you before you went home."

Ken sat back down and motioned his father toward the nearest chair. "Well, today was quite a day," he said. "I guess I needed to sit quietly for a while and kind of soak things in before I go back to the house with Janet and the kids."

His dad nodded, then aimed an approving look at Ken. "I mainly just wanted to tell you that I've never been prouder of you than I am today, especially after the service this morning."

Ken smiled. "Thanks, Dad. That means a lot."

"When you and Margie Roberson were praying over our new

missionaries, I felt my heart filling up. I know how hard it was to get the church to the point of making the commitment to send them, and I know how carefully you laid out the process to get us here. But it was a long way from where we started to where we are today, and I hope you know that God has used your natural inclination for analysis to help Gilead Bible Church reach this milestone. This wouldn't have happened without your leadership, son, and I am so happy to have been able to witness it all, from start to finish."

Ken closed his eyes and said a silent prayer of gratitude. "Well, we're not finished, Dad. Not exactly."

"I know, I know. There will be new goals, new challenges, new blessings. It doesn't stop here. But let's not forget to savor this moment. And to thank God for it."

"Yes, sir. I am. And I have been."

Ken's dad nodded, smiling. "Well, I'll get going." He stood. "And just between you and me—I'm glad you decided you didn't want to be an accountant, instead."

Ken grinned as he looked up at his father. "Me, too."

The Church Benefits from a Skilled Overseer

Challenging times demand leaders with vision and resilience. As we look through the pages of history, we can observe when harrowing events surfaced leaders who were able to seize the imaginations, minds, and hearts of their people to forge a path through the chaos. One need only think of individuals like Abraham Lincoln, Winston Churchill, Mahatma Gandhi, or Martin Luther King Jr., to realize that often, the most desperate circumstances call forth those truly outstanding persons with the fortitude, vision, and selflessness to reshape the destinies of entire nations.

I truly believe that many churches today are in difficult straits. But at the same time, I hold fast to the promise of Jesus that "heaven and earth shall pass away, but my words shall not pass away" (Matthew 24:35) and that even the gates of Hell will not prevail against the church. Because the promise of Christ is sure, He is raising up overseers through the power of His Holy Spirit to lead churches throughout the world back to their commitment to discipleship and to taking the word of salvation to every corner of the globe.

So many churches today are merely existing, and the tragedy is that they have the potential to become true Kingdom outposts in their communities. However, a skilled overseer who is well attuned to the strengths, weaknesses, talents, resources, and attitudes of the local church is uniquely able to unleash the true ministry potential of that church. The overseer possesses the skills and abilities to analyze, assess, develop processes, set goals, marshal others to take up the needed work, and identify, develop, and equip other leaders who can embrace responsibility for the mission. In doing so, the overseer serves the church as both an architect and a guide. He designs the path forward, based on the vision God has placed on his heart, and then he places the feet of his flock on that path and ensures that they pursue it until they reach their destination.

No other role in the church has the same capabilities or potential as the overseer. That is why the church must rediscover the role of the overseer and receive the work overseers do as they serve the church and reverse the decline of Western Christianity. Only when our churches are led by skilled, perceptive, Spirit-empowered overseers can they begin to achieve their true potential for bringing the light of Christ to their communities.

The Overseer and Adaptive Leadership

Because the journey to church revitalization is such a dynamic process, where assumptions must be re-assessed almost constantly in light of changing circumstances and evolving opportunities and challenges, overseers must exercise adaptive leadership. They must be able to respond quickly and decisively to shifts in the church and the community, recognizing that the former status quo is insufficient for maintaining forward progress in the mission. They must also have the resilience and fortitude to not only endure losses and setbacks but actually incorporate them into the leadership matrix, creating opportunities for growth and understanding.

This, of course, requires that adaptive leaders possess high degrees of stamina, because sustaining a confident, forward-looking leadership posture throughout the ups and downs of the five- to seven-year revitalization process can be emotionally, spiritually, and even physically draining. They must be able to both learn and unlearn, as required by the needs of the mission. In cases where they must lead through experiences of loss, adaptive leaders will need to know when it is time to let go of the previous assumptions and methods, unburdening themselves of what is no longer needed or helpful in order to move ahead with fresh understanding and revised strategic direction.

As they maintain forward momentum in ever-changing circumstances, adaptive leaders must also recognize the cognitive dissonance that their followers will experience as the church embraces ways of doing, thinking, and being that will seem unfamiliar and even intimidating. Adaptive leadership will, in other words, sometimes necessitate challenging the long-held beliefs and assumptions of some church members. Frequently, challenging such beliefs will surface strong resistance, and some truly entrenched church members may even resort to sabotage in order to derail a mission they perceive as threatening.

Despite such resistance, adaptive leaders remain steady, resisting the temptation to lose their courage or compromise on the steps needed to achieve the mission God has placed before the church. At the same time, they are able to remain vulnerable and tender-hearted toward those they are leading, rather than becoming hardened and insensitive. They exhibit calm confidence, remaining connected to those they serve as they stay the course and enable others to do the same.

"... and Father, we pray that everyone who comes to Hope Center will find not only help for the struggles they're facing, but ultimately, that they will come to know Your love, which never fails. Bless this place, bless the people who minister here in Your name, and bless those who come here seeking help. Lord, this is our effort to offer a cup of water in Your name: to feed the hungry and clothe the naked. Bear witness to our efforts, Lord, and guide us to serve as Jesus served. We ask all this in His name and for His sake, amen."

As Pastor Thomas opened his eyes and looked up at the people standing in the newly refurbished Hope Center building, he could not help but reflect on the journey that had brought Sanford Memorial

Church to this day. Thinking back to seven years ago, as he sat in his study and pondered the church's meager balance sheet, it was somewhat hard to believe that the church had been able to execute a long-term lease on what had been a slightly rundown warehouse in the industrial district near the church; to rehabilitate it with sleeping quarters, showers, an office, and classroom space; and to recruit and train a part-time director and volunteers who were now qualified to provide vocational advising, temporary housing for families facing homelessness, and referrals to appropriate social service providers. The church had even managed to identify a local licensed social worker who would offer pro bono counseling services to residents of the center who required it.

Jim Thomas had worked carefully and methodically to also create a curriculum and strategy for offering the Gospel to everyone who came to Hope Center. He had spent hours upon hours, meeting with the church members who would staff the center and discussing the most appropriate, loving, and respectful ways to offer the Word of Life along with basic food, shelter, and assistance. The people who would see to the practical and administrative needs of Hope Center were also well equipped to maintain its all-important spiritual purpose.

And now, Hope Center was a reality: a place, in the words of Esther Callan, where people would be cared for and helped to follow Jesus. Through difficult days and more than a few hard conversations, Pastor Jim had nevertheless persisted in keeping the vision in front of the members of the church. Over time, the vision and mission had taken hold in the minds and hearts of the people. Their growing enthusiasm attracted others of like mind to the church, and the mounting commitment of members was reflected in increased giving and better attitudes toward financial stewardship. As membership numbers and commitment to tithing grew, so did the ability of the church to offer improved nurture, teaching, and mentoring in discipleship. And all of it was driven by the empowering vision. Pastor

Thomas found himself remembering the often-quoted words of John Wesley: "Light yourself on fire with passion, and people will come from miles around to watch you burn." Many of those people were here today, attending the dedication of Hope Center.

Pastor Thomas's reflections were interrupted by someone touching his elbow.

"This is really something, isn't it?" said Robert McCormick, looking out over the crowd that was still milling about after the conclusion of the dedication ceremony.

"It sure is, Robert. We've come a long way, with God's help."

Robert nodded and smiled sheepishly. "I guess I have, too, since that day we met in your office and I thought we wouldn't be able to finish building the tower."

Jim grinned. "Robert, you're not the first one who has ever wondered if God had bitten off more than we could chew. And you're here today, which is what matters the most."

"I guess so." A moment later, McCormick said softly, "I just wish Esther could have lived to see it."

"Robert, I think she's smiling down on us, right now. Don't you?"

McCormick nodded thoughtfully. "Yes, I imagine you're right."

The Bible Shows the Path to Revitalization

As we bring this discussion to a close, I want to go back to what I consider the bedrock of the *ReFocus* process and its place in the revitalization of the church: It is rooted in biblical principles. Each step takes its inspiration and implementation from biblical example and precedent.

THE DISCOVERY—Beginning with the examples of Nehemiah (especially chapters 1 and 2), Josiah (2 Chronicles 34), and Joseph (Genesis 41–42), the *Discovery* uses biblical admonition to help overseers become deeply and intimately aware of the spiritual condition of their churches, especially in terms of what must be done to set the church on its journey toward revitalization.

THE CONVERGENCE—Revelation chapters 2 and 3 provide clear indications of the desire of the risen Christ for his church to be about the business of building and extending his Kingdom. Presented as the last word in Scripture, the Lord's pronouncements to the seven churches demonstrate the urgency of the overseer's task of repositioning the local church for its vital next stage of growth in discipleship.

THE PYRAMID *(Mission, Values, and Strategy)*— Inspired and driven by the final, overarching command of Jesus, the mission of the revitalized church (What do we do?) is clear: "... Go, therefore, and make disciples of all nations" (Matthew 28:19). The values toward which the overseer will guide the church (Why do we do it?) are taken directly from those most treasured by the earliest Christians as recorded in Acts 2:42–47: worship, evangelism, discipleship, ministry, fellowship, stewardship, generosity, and prayer. The strategy (How do we do it?) is found by examining Jesus' own methods for calling, forming, and sending followers, as exemplified by *The Path*.

THE PATH—Revitalized churches follow the path for making disciples that Jesus established when He called, formed, and sent out His disciples: "Come and see" (John 1:46), "Follow me" (Matthew 4:19), "Abide in me," (John 15:7), "Go and tell" (Luke 8:38–39). As overseers follow this same path, they must pray for the wisdom, creativity, and passion provided by the Holy Spirit, just as Jesus promised His followers in Luke 24:49 ("... you will be clothed with power from on high").

THE LADDER—Just as Jesus formed His followers into powerful messengers for the Kingdom, overseers will gather and empower others to become channels for the vital work of discipleship. Internalizing the principles outlined by Paul in Philippians 2:19–30, overseers will both exemplify and form in others the heart of a leader— concern for others, safeguarding the interests of Jesus, reliability, and commitment to advancing the Gospel. They will also cultivate and instill in others the habits of spiritual leadership: loyalty, a strong work ethic, courage, effective communication, and pastoral care. Finally, they will both receive and provide the honor due to faithful spiritual leaders by rejoicing in their victories, receiving them with joy, and risking opposition to maintain the integrity of the mission.

THE TOOLKIT—Overseers are equipped to carry out the work of revitalization by using tools and methods founded in the scriptural principles shown above. These biblically based, field-tested tools will support overseers as they set about changing the culture of the church, casting and implementing vision, managing systems, and aligning their churches for becoming full participants in the advancement of the Great Commission.

Moving beyond Limitations into Revitalization

If the church is to fully realize its potential—and to carry out its final and greatest commission from the Lord—overseers will need to arise and capture the bold vision of Christ. This will require them to overcome the limitations imposed by lack of adequate training, gaps in understanding, or hesitancy about seizing the roles demanded to fully carry out the God-given task of providing true, transformative oversight for their churches.

But God's call is clear. Christ's vision for his church is unequivocal. And the required methods, actions, and processes are available. As a pastor of God's people, you can learn how to be an overseer. You can apply these principles to your unique pastoral setting and undertake the vital work of moving your church toward revitalization.

The way forward lies in front of you. What is the next step of faith that God is calling you to take?

Notes

1. World Economic Forum, "Outlook on the Global Agenda, 2015," available at https://www3.weforum.org/docs/GAC14/WEF_GAC14_OutlookGlobalAgenda_Report.pdf

Tools for Overseers

As part of its mission to help leaders revitalize the church, Corpus has developed, field-tested, and refined a series of tools, assessments, and implementation resources, many of which you can find in this appendix. These instruments can be used to evaluate the pastor's readiness for leading change as well as the church's vision receptivity toward the changes needed for revitalization. The appendix also offers an overview of other tools to help pastors revitalize their church. As you look at these tools, we hope you can imagine them being deployed in your church to help you know if revitalization can be accomplished, how hard the revitalization process might be, and where the challenges to revitalization exist. Knowing all of this greatly enhances the likelihood that a pastor can lead a revitalization. If you are a pastor or church leader looking for a place to begin, we always recommend the PRA *(Pastoral Readiness Assessment)* and the VRA *(Vision Receptivity Assessment)* because these assessments will provide you with the necessary feedback you need before anything else.

> Our prayer and belief is that overseers will find here the support and guidance needed to successfully lead their congregations in revitalization.

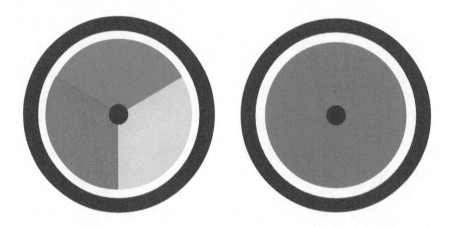

Pastoral Readiness Assessment

Apart from God, His Word, and His Spirit, the greatest single influence upon a church is its pastor. The pastor's character, competency, teaching, and daily interaction with the church and staff, along with the pastor's theology and priorities in ministry, will shape a church more than anything else.

Pastors who intentionally lead through the church renewal process must have an especially well-honed skillset. These skills can be categorized into three biblical roles (elder, shepherd, and overseer), each specifically developed to meet the unique challenges of church revitalization. At Corpus, we have intentionally added a descriptor to the three biblical titles a pastor bears. The pastor must be 1) a *wise* elder; 2) a *strategic* overseer; and 3) a *transformational* shepherd.

All three of these roles have special subsets of skills that a revitalizing pastor must possess in order to increase the likelihood of a successful church revitalization. Even pastors who do not feel skilled in these areas are able to grow into them through education, training, coaching, and intentional development.

The *Pastoral Readiness Assessment* (PRA) consists of three parts: 1) a questionnaire; 2) a graph to help evaluate and visualize your questionnaire results; and 3) a coaching plan for development. (See examples to follow: *Images 20–22.*)

The Questionnaire

Divided into three sections, one for each of the pastoral roles, the questionnaire has three sets of ten statements in each section. Pastors should score each statement on a scale from 1 (lowest) to 10 (highest). Scores for each section are computed and averaged. The accuracy and usefulness of the assessment are dependent upon the pastor's self-awareness and honesty. This assessment can be taken by an individual or, for best results, it can be taken as a 360° assessment (as shown in the example *Image 23)* to include feedback from other, trusted persons in the church.

APPENDIX

Pastoral Readiness Assessment | Questionnaire

ROLE 2 | SKILLED OVERSEER

Write your score for each statement in the "Score"column, with 10 as the highest agreement, and 1 as the lowest.

SKILLSET 4 - Leads a Change Process	SCORE
The pastor sees where the church needs to go and is able to take steps in that direction.	8
The pastor is able to assess accurately the current reality in the church.	6
The pastor challenges people to try new and innovative ways of doing things.	5
The pastor knows and communicates how all of the church's ministries are interconnected.	7
The pastor can easily and consistently answer the directional questions of the church.	8
The pastor seeks out challenges and opportunities for the church.	5
The pastor seeks to learn from other pastors and churches in order to do ministry better.	9
The pastor knows how to develop people and use them in the work of the ministry.	8
The pastor knows how to implement changes.	6
The pastor knows how fast or how slow to move in order to be successful in leading change.	8
Add statement scores to get SKILLSET 4 Total _____ ; divide this number by 10 to get your SKILLSET 4 AVERAGE →	7.0

SKILLSET 5 - Casts Vision and Implements Strategy	
The pastor is able to paint the big picture for the future of the church.	10
The pastor has a clearly-articulated plan to help the church take its next step.	9
The pastor knows how the church needs to execute its ministry.	8
The pastor develops cooperative relationships within the church so that more tasks can be accomplished.	7
The pastor has taken the time to cast vision and articulate a strategy.	8
The pastor is often described as a strategic thinker.	7
The pastor can see the bigger picture of the church's ministry while also working on the smaller individual parts.	8
The pastor knows how to allocate resources to accomplish the work of the ministry.	8
The pastor is knowledgeable about vision and strategy.	10
The pastor is able to evaluate how effectively the vision is being implemented.	7
Add statement scores to get SKILLSET 5 Total _____ ; divide this number by 10 to get your SKILLSET 5 AVERAGE →	8.2

SKILLSET 6 - Aligns Resources and Executes Daily	
The pastor knows how to prioritize time and appointments to accomplish the most important responsibilities in the church.	5
The pastor knows how to assign tasks and hold people accountable for their ministry.	4
The pastor understands how the things done each day are linked to the long-term vision of the church.	4
The pastor helps people do their ministry better.	3
The pastor ensures that people grow and mature through the ministry they perform.	6
The pastor knows how to support and encourage people while they are performing the work of the ministry.	4
The pastor knows how to get things done through others.	3
The pastor regularly acknowledges the contributions of others and says thank you.	7
The pastor understands the projects assigned to staff/lay leaders and walks beside them as they work.	4
The pastor helps secure resources to make sure the tasks can be accomplished.	3
Add statement scores to get SKILLSET 6 Total _____ ; divide this number by 10 to get your SKILLSET 6 AVERAGE →	4.3

(Image 20)

Pastoral Readiness Assessment | Summary Graph Examples

The greater the coverage, the greater the likelihood that revitalization can take place.

Strengths can be identified that can assist a pastor in the revitalization effort.

_____
_____
_____
_____
_____
_____

The less coverage, the less likely that revitalization can take place.

Potential blind spots can be identified where the pitfalls to revitalization can occur.

_____
_____
_____
_____
_____
_____

(Image 21)

COACHING CERTIFICATION | PRA Coaching Plan

Casts Vision & Implements Strategy

Definition
Pastors must be able to see a preferred future with wisdom and spiritual insight and guide the church to fulfill its mission by accomplishing the individual steps of its strategy. This requires the pastor to see the future, know the steps to get there, and work to refine those steps until they are perfected and impactful.

Resources
Aubrey Malphours, *Advanced Strategic Planning*
David C. Cook, *Relaunch How to Stage an Organizational Comeback*
Will Mancini, *Church Unique*

Strengths
Most leaders have a natural bias towards focusing on either vision or strategy. A church revitalizer must have both. A church in need of revitalization is most likely in that condition because its vision has been lost and its strategy is not working. The leader who has developed the skills of both vision and strategy is a rare person, but almost always an effective leader.

Struggles
If the pastor's assessment indicates they need to develop this category of their toolkit in order to become a church revitalizer, they will need to learn how to effectively describe where they are leading the church and what steps they are going to take to get there. Having a clear vision will help them identify where they are seeking to lead the church, and knowing the strategy they are following will help them not only move forward, but also know what to do when they lose their way. Refer to the grid below to help the pastor you are coaching develop these interdependent skills.

DEVELOPMENTAL PLAN		
GOAL 1: *Score 4.3*		
BEHAVIORAL CHANGES:		
What behavioral changes would you like to achieve?	*Learn the basic skills of vision casting and strategy development.*	
MY ACTION PLAN: Strategies & Action Steps	INVOLVEMENT OF OTHERS	TARGET DATE
Read resources.	*Discuss with Coach*	*Jan – March 2018*
Develop a preliminary strategy and experiment with describing it and using it.	*Church leaders and teachers*	*March – Dec 2018*

(Image 22)

Pastoral Readiness Assessment | 360° Scores

If you are taking this assessment to participate in a 360° evaluation of a pastor, score each statement as an evaluation of the skill or ability of the pastor. All of the averages and shading of the graph should be completed based on the 360° averages, not the participant's scores alone.

PARTICIPANT AVERAGES	PASTOR	COLLEAGUE	COLLEAGUE	BOARD MEMBER	BOARD MEMBER	CHURCH PARTICIPANT	CHURCH PARTICIPANT	AVERAGE FROM 360°
Skillset #1 Seeks God and Leads People	7.1	6.5	6.7	5.6	5.8	6.0	5.9	6.2
Skillset #2 Character that Builds Trust	4.2	5.9	5.3	4.7	4.9	6.5	6.9	5.5
Skillset #3 Communication that Inspires	7.7	8.1	8.2	7.6	7.3	9.2	8.9	8.1
Skillset #4 Leads a Change Process	7.0	6.8	6.9	6.4	6.1	6.7	6.9	6.7
Skillset #5 Casts Vision & Implements Strategy	8.2	8.7	9.1	7.7	7.3	8.4	8.7	8.3
Skillset #6 Alignment & Execution	4.3	5.2	5.4	5.1	6.0	5.3	6.1	5.3
Skillset #7 Loves and Cares for People	7.3	7.5	6.9	6.1	5.8	6.7	7.1	6.8
Skillset #8 Gathers & Influences People	6.7	6.6	6.8	7.0	7.2	7.1	7.3	7.0
Skillset #9 Corrects Misplaced Values	4.9	5.4	6.1	4.3	4.8	6.5	6.3	5.5

(Image 23)

Church Vision Receptivity Assessment

Culture is more powerful than vision and strategy combined. Awareness of your church's existing culture will help you know how diligent you must be during vision implementation. The *Vision Receptivity Assessment* (VRA) is designed to help pastors evaluate how receptive the existing church culture is toward the new vision being cast. (See examples to follow: *Images 24–25.*)

The Questionnaire

You, along with a group of other church leaders, will complete this exercise by scoring ten statements on a continuum in nine different categories that describe church culture. Corpus will then plot the averages on a graph to create a visual representation of how receptive your church is toward the new vision. The greater the coverage on the graph, the higher the likelihood that the revitalization vision will be received. Conversely, the less coverage, the more challenging it will be to cast the vision into the existing culture (refer to *Image 15*, pg. 142). The results will also provide pastors with insight into specific areas of cultural challenges faced by the church. A Corpus-certified coach can work with a pastor to address the challenging aspects of the church culture.

To complete the Pastoral Readiness Assessment (PRA) and the Vision Receptivity Assessment (VRA) or to discover the other assessments Corpus offers to help you move forward in revitalizing your ministry, scan the QR Code.

Vision Receptivity Assessment

In the table below, compile your score for each section as well as the scores of everyone else on your team. Then calculate and record the average score for each section in the last column. You will use these average scores to complete the graph on the next page.

PARTICIPANT NAME	Jennifer	Evan	JC	Nate	Tommy	Rody	Rick	Davis	Jacob		AVERAGE
On Mission v. Religious Activity	7.7	6.2	7.4	7.0	7.2	6.6	6.6	6.3	5.6		**6.7**
Courage v. Fear	8.3	6.4	6.9	6.9	7.8	8.6	7.2	8.4	6.9		**7.5**
Trust v. Distrust	6.5	4.1	7.2	5.3	6.1	7.6	4.2	5.1	7.3		**5.9**
Authentic Communication v. Withheld Information	5.9	5.0	5.8	7.5	7.2	5.6	6.1	6.8	5.7		**6.1**
Clarity v. Chaos	7.5	5.9	6.7	8.7	7.7	7.6	6.6	8.0	7.0		**7.3**
Adaptive v. Inflexible	8.2	6.6	6.6	6.6	7.9	7.8	5.7	7.0	6.2		**6.9**
Joyful v. Negative	7.9	6.4	7.9	9.1	8.2	8.0	6.6	8.0	7.6		**7.7**
Empowering v. Controlling	8.6	8.3	7.8	8.4	8.0	9.1	6.5	7.7	7.7		**8.0**
Honesty v. Deception	7.9	6.0	6.4	8.9	7.4	7.1	6.7	8.2	7.5		**7.3**

(Image 24)

Vision Receptivity Assessment

SECTION 6: ADAPTIVE VERSUS INFLEXIBLE	SCORE
The church tries new things readily.	
Church leadership is excited about regularly bringing new ideas to the church.	
Those who are resistant to new ideas feel pressure to change.	
The statement "that is not how we do things here" is rarely used.	
The church is willing to adapt to the needs of the community around it.	
The church views its programs as a means to do ministry and not as something sacred they have always done.	
The church is generally positive about embracing new ideas.	
When a new staff member comes to the church, his or her ideas are readily embraced.	
The church is generally on the cutting edge of ministry.	
Lay leaders are open to being redirected by staff members with new ideas.	
TOTAL SECTION SCORE	
DIVIDED BY 10	8.2

SECTION 7: JOYFUL VERSUS NEGATIVE	SCORE
The church is a happy place for people to come.	
The church refuses to be a place of negativity.	
Gossip and backbiting are quickly rejected.	
The church is quick to celebrate what God is obviously doing.	
The church is marked by smiles, friendship, and hope.	
Cynical people are quickly corrected and expected to change their attitudes.	
Critical people are confronted and challenged to get on board with the church's mission.	
The church services are marked by engagement, responsiveness, and laughter.	
Church members quickly receive new members and welcome them into the church.	
New members quickly catch the culture of joy, warmth, and love.	
TOTAL SECTION SCORE	
DIVIDED BY 10	7.9

(Image 25)

Cultural Assessment Overview

The culture of your church will exert outsized influence on the vision and strategy you develop for moving the church toward revitalization. The cultural assessment tool shown below is designed to help you evaluate existing culture and help you identify what needs to be added to or removed from the church culture. A portion of *The Toolkit* in the *ReFocus* process addresses how to identify the contributors to detracting aspects of the church culture and provides you the opportunity to identify replacement parts that contribute to a more receptive culture.

EXISTING CULTURE						
ATTITUDE	+	BELIEFS & BEHAVIOR	+	CUSTOMS	=	CULTURE

ADDITIONS TO THE CULTURE			

(Image 26)

The Toolkit, an Overview

These carefully designed tools will help pastors gain information and insights, develop plans for implementation and communication, and build strategies for leadership development and discipleship training in their churches. In addition to the pastoral and church readiness assessments already discussed (and also listed below), the *ReFocus Toolkit* contains resources in the following vital areas:

Culture

◇ Vision Receptivity

◇ Culture Assessment

Implementation Plan

◇ Vision and Launch Implementation/Leadership Summit/ Vision Summary Handout

◇ Preaching Plan

◇ Building Momentum: Celebrating Early Wins

◇ Process and Pace of Vision Adoption (charting progress)

Systems Management

◇ Systems Management Checklist

◇ Communications Calendars

◇ Pastoral Care/Congregational Ministry

Alignment

◇ Meaningful Meetings

◇ Staff Evaluation and Performance Plan

◇ Coaching Questions

◇ Annual Plan

◇ Making Hard Decisions

◇ Conflict Management Resource

◇ Building Trust

◇ Staff Retreat Agenda Examples

◇ New Members/Guest Orientation

◇ Staff and Pastoral Team Agendas

◇ Planning Worship Services

◇ Giving Ladder

◇ Multi-Site Strategy (for churches with multiple campuses)

Roadmap Example

Presented here on the following pages is a hypothetical example of how the *ReFocus* process might look at a particular local church, "Hickorywood Church." Based on an amalgamation of data and responses gathered from various churches experiencing revitalization, this fictional church *ReFocus* plan offers a bird's-eye view of how each of the six phases in the revitalization journey might look in a local church context.

THE ROAD MAP | Individualized ReFocus Church Plan

Church's Name: **Hickorywood Baptist Church**

THE DISCOVERY

Our Five Core Discoveries are:

1. Trust - Develop a culture of trust so the church can function effectively and pursue its God-given mission.

2. Leadership - Develop a comprehensive church-wide approach to identifying and developing new leaders.

3. Vision - must reignite its spiritual passion by committing itself to a common vision that inspires individual members.

4. Facilities - Hickorywood must plan for and create space to accommodate growth including first impressions, women's restrooms, parking, and worship space.

5. Plan - Hickorywood must create a comprehensive plan for moving forward year by year so we don not grow stagnant.

THE CONVERGENCE

Our Big Idea is:

We believe God desires Hickorywood to: Bridge/Brokenness

REFOCUS

THE ROAD MAP | Individualized ReFocus Church Plan

THE PYRAMID

Our MISSION is:

Sharing Christ by building relationships through serving our community.

Our VALUES are:

1. Family - We value God's design & purpose for the family.
2. Worship - We value engaging people in a vibrant walk with God.
3. Encouragement - We value sharing source of our hope with everyone.
4. Generosity - We value using our time, talent & treasure to glorify God.
5. Prayer - We value prayer as foundational amongst God's children.
6. Ministry/Service - We value ministry through serving others.

The steps in our STRATEGY are:

1. Connecting to God through worship and to one another in fellowship.
2. Growing in our faith through intentional discipleship.
3. Serving the church and community through ministry.
4. Going and fulfilling the Great Commission through evangelism and missions.

THE ROAD MAP | Individualized ReFocus Church Plan

THE PYRAMID (continued)

The VISION of our church is to:

Develop disciples to be the Bridge for Connecting the Broken to Christ.

To fulfill this vision, the church must:

1. Build a discipleship pipeline that grows mature followers of Jesus.

2. Train members to engage lostness so individual members live missionally.

3. Launch a leadership ladder that equips members to take on more responsibility for ministry within the church.

4. Develop a master plan to address facilities needs.

5. Train members in generosity through a capital campaign that gives the church opportunity to sacrifice.

THE ROAD MAP | Individualized ReFocus Church Plan

THE PYRAMID (continued)

The focus for this year's ANNUAL PLAN is:

Build a discipleship pipeline.

The elements in our ANNUAL PLAN are:

1. Launch Sunday School under a new name to engage the next generation.
2. Train leaders to launch 4 new classes.
3. Implement new members class and next steps class to move visitors into Sunday School.
4. Create a devotional plan to engage Sunday School participants in daily Bible engagement.
5. Establish mentoring relationships based on interest.

The GOALS for our church are:

1. Build members into mature disciples of Jesus.
2. Increase baptisms and membership as a result of our participation in personal missional engagement.
3. Double the number of leaders in the church to overcome the leadership deficit within the church and 50% of the new leaders must be under the age of 40.
4. Develop a master plan that doubles the size of the existing church.
5. Raise $1.5 M to build the new ministry space.

THE ROAD MAP | Individualized ReFocus Church Plan

THE PATH

The steps in our PATH for evangelism and discipleship are:

1. CONNECT to God through worship & others through fellowship.
2. GROW in our faith through intentional discipleship.
3. SERVE the church & community through ministry.
4. GO and fulfill the Great Commission through evangelism & missions.

A picture of our plan is:

THE LADDER

We will develop leaders by:

1. Lead self - Teaching leadership principles to those identified as having leadership potential.
2. Leading teams - mentoring those already serving in a leadership role so they can be more effective and impactful through their leadership.
3. Leading leaders - develop this level of leadership so the leadership burden of the church is shared and the footprint of the church can grow.
4. Leading the church - train the leaders of the church to envision all of the church ministry and not simply represent a portion of the church.

REF**O**CUS

THE ROAD MAP | Individualized ReFocus Church Plan

THE TOOLKIT

We will use these tools to implement our *ReFocus* plan:

1. Sermon series that unrolls the vision, titled: Bridges

2. A "Leadership Summit"where we train our staff and leaders.

3. Weekly meetings with {participants} that address the annual plan weekly, and the goals monthly. Meetings with church council and deacons to set monthly objects and hold one another accountable.

4. The development of a budget and church calendar that is driven by the mission, vision and annual plan. Starting with the church budget in August, budget for the new priorities this vision sets.

5. Training Sunday School teachers in the path for disciple-making.

6. Teaching the church leadership how to develop leaders through monthly meetings on: Leadership training will be held each Wed. pm through the Fall.

APPENDIX

Certification and Multiplication of Ministry

Arising from our deep commitment to equip pastors for the task of leading churches in revitalization and out of our desire to create a worldwide movement of revitalization, Corpus has designed courses and certifications to meet a variety of needs. These include providing individual support through assessment, coaching, and/or using our Corpus resources at the church, associational, network, or denominational level. Corpus has developed certification models that build out the principles discussed in this book. Upon your certification, you will be able to offer these resources through your ministry.

Certifications include:

1. **READINESS AND RECEPTIVITY ASSESSMENTS AND COACHING CERTIFICATION**—trains a coach to give and score the VRA and PRA and to coach the pastors/leaders who are assessed from the results;

2. **PATHFINDER CERTIFICATION**—training for pastors/leaders who want to lead a church through the six steps of revitalization described in the book;

3. **LEADER RESILIENCE ASSESSMENT AND COACHING CERTIFICATION**—trains coaches to walk beside a pastor throughout the three to seven years required to see revitalization occur;

4. **TRANSITIONAL REVITALIZATION PASTOR CERTIFICATION**—designed to help transitional pastors initiate the work of church revitalization during an interim.

5. **REVITALIZATION PASTOR CERTIFICATION**—designed as a continuing education model for pastors to be able to represent themselves to prospective churches as competent in the six skills of the overseer.

Scan the QR Code to learn more about upcoming Corpus training and certification events.

Bibliography

Personal Preparation for Vision Casting
- ◊ Patrick Lencioni, *The Motive*
- ◊ Eugene H. Peterson, *Run with the Horses: The Quest for Life at Its Best*
- ◊ Ben Arment, *Dream Year*
- ◊ Gary Keller and Jay Papasan, *The ONE Thing: The Surprisingly Simple Truth Behind Extraordinary Results*

Dealing with Difficulty in Revitalization
- ◊ Gary Thomas, *When to Walk Away: Finding Freedom from Toxic People*
- ◊ Angela Duckworth, *Grit: The Power of Passion and Perseverance*
- ◊ Henri J.M. Nouwen, *The Wounded Healer: Ministry in Contemporary Society*

Master Planning in Churches
- ◊ Aubrey Malphurs, *Advanced Strategic Planning*
- ◊ Will Mancini, *Church Unique*

Organizational Development
- ◊ Patrick Lencioni, *Silos, Politics, and Turf Wars*
- ◊ Patrick Lencioni, *The Advantage*
- ◊ Patrick Lencioni, *The Ideal Team Player*
- ◊ Simon Sinek, *Start with Why: How Great Leaders Inspire Everyone to Take Action*

Meetings
- ◊ Patrick Lencioni, *The Five Dysfunctions of a Team*
- ◊ Patrick Lencioni, *Death by Meeting*

BIBLIOGRAPHY

Strategy
- ◇ Jim Collins, *Turning The Flywheel*
- ◇ Les McKeown, *Predictable Success*
- ◇ John Doerr and Larry Page, *Measure What Matters*

Mission Clarity and Development
- ◇ Peter Greer and Chris Horst, *Mission Drift*

Vision Development
- ◇ Will Mancini, *God Dreams*
- ◇ Os Guinness, *The Call: Finding and Fulfilling God's Purpose for Your Life*
- ◇ Michael Hyatt, *The Vision Driven Leader*

Leadership Development
- ◇ Ram Cheran, Stephen Drotter, and James Noel, *Leadership Pipeline*
- ◇ Gordon McDonald, *Who Stole My Church: What to Do when the Church You Love Tries to Enter the 21st Century*
- ◇ J. Robert Clinton, *The Making of a Leader*

Coaching
- ◇ Keith Webb, *The Coach Model*
- ◇ Bob Logan, *Coaching 101*

Culture
- ◇ Samuel Chand, *Cracking Your Church's Culture Code*
- ◇ Robert Lewis and Wayne Cordeiro, *Culture Shift*
- ◇ John P. Kotter, *Leading Change*
- ◇ Mark Rutland, *Relaunch: How to Stage an Organizational Turnaround*
- ◇ Tod Bolsinger, *Canoeing the Mountains: Christian Leadership in Uncharted Territory*

- ◇ Daniel Coyle, *The Culture Code: The Secrets of Highly Successful Groups*

Preaching for Revitalization

- ◇ Andrew M. Davis and Mark Dever, *Revitalize: Biblical Keys to Helping Your Church Come Alive Again*

Shepherding for Revitalization

- ◇ Brian Croft, *Biblical Church Revitalization: Solutions for Dying & Divided Churches (Practical Shepherding)*

Revitalization

- ◇ Aubrey Malphurs and Gordon Penfold, *Revision: The Key to Transforming Your Church*
- ◇ Bob Buford, *Halftime: Moving from Success to Significance*

About the Author

Dr. Rob Peters

Rob is a graduate of Tennessee Tech, Southwestern Seminary, and Southeastern Seminary. He worked at Deloitte and at Ernst & Young in the accounting and consulting fields prior to entering the ministry. He has served as the senior pastor at three churches of varying sizes for more than 25 years.

Rob is the founder and president of Corpus, a global church revitalization ministry. Corpus envisions a world filled with vibrant churches impacting their communities for Christ as we work to equip church leaders with the biblical leadership skills necessary to reignite the church's mission and enhance congregational health.

Rob has been married to Wendy for more than 25 years, and they have three children.

To discover the state of your ministry and whether you need to revitalize, scan the QR code for a quick **FREE Assessment.**

Please visit ***www.TheOverseer.info*** *for more information.*

Made in the USA
Columbia, SC
06 November 2023

24939028R20135